WORSHIP LEADERSHIP
FOR WORSHIP LEADERS

VOL. 1: DEVELOPING EFFECTIVE LEADERSHIP SKILLS

WILLIAM L. HOOPER

A Follow *Me!* Book
An imprint of Alexander Publishing
PO Box 1720, Petersburg, VA 23805

CONTENTS

FOREWORD

DAN MCLAUGHLIN

A s a teenager I came to understand and believe in a principle that still guides me in my spiritual life: rather than focusing on my individual behaviors and trying to do all the right things (avoiding the wrong things), it is much more effective to get my attitude "screwed on straight," and let that attitude or spirit lead me to the kind of right behaviors that I want in my life.

Here are two scriptures that embody to me this inside-out sort of transformation:

Do not conform any longer to the pattern of this world, but be transformed by the renewing of your mind. Then you will be able to test and approve what God's will is—his good, pleasing and perfect will. (Romans 12:2, NIV)

Trust in the LORD with all your heart
*   and lean not on your own understanding;*
in all your ways acknowledge him,
*   and he will make your paths straight.* (Proverbs 3:5-6, NIV)

In recent years, Rick Warren's *Purpose Driven* books have been another example of the application of this principle.

That same principle, applied to music ministry, is what will make *Worship Leadership For Worship Leaders* so valuable to anyone aspiring to minister through music. It is all about letting the "why" lead us to the "what."

Wisely allowing considerable room for differences that can arise between the situations of different music ministers, Dr. Hooper focuses in many sections more on raising questions than on giving pat answers. Some may find this approach frustrating (it makes you think!), but it allows the book a broader usefulness and application.

In the end, these unanswered questions are not questions of universal Truth about the nature of God, man, sin, and redemption, but rather questions of personal values or one's approach to one's own situation. In many cases, they are simply questions of culture, not Gospel Truth. Far too much energy has been expended in churches arguing passionately about questions of culture as if they were Gospel. This is not to say questions of culture don't deserve our attention. They do, but we need not treat our answers in these cases as universal truths.

In any case, answering the questions Dr. Hooper raises will develop a sort of "ministry values system" that can guide a music minister naturally toward the most important things to be done, and how to do them. And having wrestled personally with them – rather than simply accepting an author's answers – will make the reader own the resulting ministry vision more fully.

As you read, you will be able to discern several things about the author. Dr. Hooper is a deep and thorough thinker, a man of God, and it is evident that he cares deeply about the subject at hand.

So, prepare yourself to get "under the hood" and examine the inner workings of your view of ministry, and let God so shape the results that you will be left with a philosophy of ministry that both aligns with the truths of God's word, and successfully applies these truths to modern culture – even church culture.

DAN McLAUGHLIN
Associate Pastor, Worship and Missions
McCarthy Baptist Church
St. Joseph, Missouri

INTRODUCTION

This book is the result of the author's many years of experience as a pastor, pastoral counselor, church musician, music teacher, and seminary professor. It has been written in the conviction that there are many areas of concern that have not been given serious thought sufficiently by those who are involved with worship leadership in a church.

Ten years of experience in England as music teacher, minister of music, and pastor have served as a catalyst to bring these many issues together. To live in a different but similar culture, and to work in a similar but different school and church situation has caused me to reassess what ministry is all about. This is because many of the assumptions and presuppositions upon which one's ministry is based in one's native land come into question in a foreign country. The conditions under which one must minister abroad make it imperative to determine what the crucial issues are.

To be the pastor or worship leader in one of the evangelical denominations of the United States is to be among the majority. In England, evangelical churches are in a minority. There is a distinct difference between the worldview of a majority and that of a minority. In order to survive, the minority must be clear in what it believes and how it lives out its faith. To move from a majority mentality to a minority mentality proved to be difficult, but rewarding to me.

I returned to the United States in 1983 to become Dean of Fine Arts at Southwest Baptist University. I discovered many changes were taking place in churches. One major change was churches adapting popular music styles and performance practices for worship music. Adapting popular music culture for worship of the church raises serious issues. My concerns were published first in 1986 in a book titled *Ministry and Musicians.* Some of the material in that book has been revised and incorporated in this book. Other sections are new. Though I have not written either for the scholar or the pastor, hopefully both scholar and pastor will find the book helpful. I have written both for the intending and practicing worship leader.

The chapter titles reflect the concerns I have for music and worship in the church. Worship leaders must think about themselves as a person; the nature of the music they use; their philosophy of music; their theology in relation to music; the role of music as a cultural reality; their task as music teachers; and their task as leaders of worship. Many things are oversimplified. Other things have been omitted. More questions are raised than are sufficiently answered, if at all. No one will be totally satisfied with the results.

I have taken this approach deliberately, for it is my conviction that all types of ministry among some denominations have become so professionalized and specialized that we are in danger of developing a state church mentality and a representative priesthood. The people become faceless pawns in a vocational chess game to the glory of the ministers. God forbid!

The book is not intended as a "how to do it" manual. Instead, its purpose is to explore those issues upon which worship leadership must be based. If what is written will cause you to think and to argue back, so much the better. If the book stimulates you to write about these same issues from another perspective, better still.

l owe a great debt to my many English friends who helped me to come to grips with what ministry is all about. Hopefully, I have also made a contribution as I ministered to and with them. I also owe a great debt to former students who dialogued with me in the classroom and challenged my thinking.

I am grateful to Peter Alexander and Alexander Publishing Company for the opportunity to let my voice be heard again.

WILLIAM L. HOOPER
Bolivar, Missouri
August 2007

CHAPTER 1

ALL ABOUT YOU
what about me is changing?

This chapter is all about you. You may be called a minister of music, a worship pastor or a worship leader. The title is not important. What is important is the kind of person you are. Little attention is given to the humanity of the person who leads worship. We put a lot of emphasis upon training, skills and performance but little attention to who this person is as a person.

Before you are anything else, you are a human being and all that means. In this chapter we will explore your humanity.

YOU ARE A PERSON

You can deny everything about yourself except your humanness. How you see yourself as a person determines how you see others and yourself in relation to others. Our evangelical emphasis upon sin and grace has caused most of us to miss part of what Jesus taught: we are to love our neighbor as our self (Matthew 19:19). What we miss is the last half; we fail to love ourselves properly. Until we have the right attitude toward self, we can never love our neighbor. The Greek phrase could mean, "to lose sight of one's own interests." To illustrate this, Jesus told the story of the Good Samaritan (Luke 9:25-38). Until we have the right attitude toward self, we can never love our neighbor.

What the New Testament means by the word *self* is not the meaning of the self given by modern psychologists. When Jesus told us to deny the self, He was talking about the ego. Jesus could not deny His self, for the self is the same as the soul (in Hebrew the word soul, also translated self, is *nephesh*). Denying the ego is necessary, for it can be destructive of the real self. From this perspective, a person is an emotional creature, a social creature, and potentially an adult.

AN EMOTIONAL CREATURE

As a human being you are an emotional creature, for God has created you that way. Just as you differ from others physically you are different emotionally. No two people respond the same way to the same experiences. Life would be very dull if we were all clones of the same person.

When you feel an emotion, there are three possible responses you can make: the emotion can be denied, it can be acted out in behavior, or it can be owned. You can neither keep emotion from welling up inside nor can you always control the circumstances that trigger your emotions. You must own your emotions, for too often a person will deny his or her feelings rather than owning them or acting them out.

If you think your feelings are bad or dangerous you will not own them. If you are afraid of the consequences of your feelings, you deny having them to avoid punishment or embarrassment. Obviously, you do not want to act out your emotions, for this can be destructive to yourself and to others. You must accept your feelings at a given moment, whether they are good, bad, or indifferent. If you accept a feeling, you can learn what to do with it the next time you have the same feeling. It is then possible to learn how to control the way you respond to an emotion you consider to be dangerous. If you know certain situations and/or people trigger feelings that cause you problems and you cannot always evade the situation, you can determine in advance what your response will be in the situation.

If you deny jealousy, you can never give of yourself. Avoid grief and you will never find or give consolation. If you are afraid to feel anger, you become less capable of love. By denying you have feelings of unforgiveness, you will never receive forgiveness or give it to others. If feelings of worry are fearful, then you are less capable of having trust. If you find it difficult to admit being lonely, then it becomes difficult to become caring of others. If you deny feelings of resentment, you will have less understanding of others. If you cannot accept moments of depression, you will never experience hope.

The fear of feeling any kind of emotions can cause us to become almost incapable of feeling anything. Many people would agree that love is a good emotion that should be felt and owned. But what if a person loves another deeply and that love is not returned? The person becomes afraid to love, for love has become a dangerous emotion.

It is good to own and to feel trust. However, if we place trust in someone only to have that trust betrayed, we will be afraid to feel trust. Who wants to be devastated by a "good" feeling that has turned "bad"?

Whenever you deny or avoid emotions, you experience a terrible effort to control them. You may become less warm and spontaneous. Your behavior becomes one of constant wariness lest your emotions control you. If you must maintain constant vigilance over your emotions, then they already control you.

You are the only one who can do anything about how you respond to deeper feelings. Your feelings may be caused by circumstances beyond your control and experienced without your consciously willing them. You cannot stop becoming angry or jealous or afraid, but you can choose to own those feelings and choose not to deny them or to act them out.

Accepting responsibility for your emotions can help you to determine how you will respond to the situation instead of reacting to it. As you learn to control your responses to feelings, you will begin to see yourself in a more favorable light. You will also discover ways to deal constructively with situations instead of permitting situations to deal with you destructively.

YOU ARE A CHRISTIAN

If you are a human being before anything else, then next you are a Christian, Perhaps this is taken for granted, but should it be? Some unknown sage has given this definition of a Christian: one who gives as much of himself as he is able to, as much of God as he can understand. This definition means a total commitment at any given time to as much of God as we understand. If we grow in our commitment to Christ, we also grow in our understanding of and relationship to Christ.

From the evangelical perspective, a Christian is one who has repented of his sin and personally asked for Christ to come into his life as Savior and Lord. However, this is not a static, one-time experience. This is a continuing experience. You must accept the fact that you are on a lifelong pilgrimage of faith just like every other believer.

YOU ARE A SOCIAL CREATURE

You are a social creature. You were not made to live in isolation from other people. Social participation and responsibility must extend beyond the church we serve. There is no retreat from life. We are to be salt and light, but if we are salt and light only to other believers it is self-destructive. Too much salt causes bitterness, and too much light causes blindness.

You are or will be involved in dating and selecting a life partner just like other persons. You must learn to adjust to, and live harmoniously with, a marriage partner. You may begin a family and will assimilate the tasks of parenting and learn how to manage a home and to assume household responsibilities.

As a member of society you are expected to embark upon a career and to assume some type of civic responsibility. You cannot use a divine calling to opt out of social responsibility and must search for congenial social groups outside the church. You cannot remove yourself from the corporate sins of mankind. You cannot submerge yourself in the church in order to escape the world; there is no escape.

YOU AIM FOR MATURITY

The church is the body of Christ, and a body must occupy space. That space is in the society of men. Christian service is to be spiritual, but it is also to be bodily. Our spiritual service must be performed in the arena of bodily day-to-day life. A church that does not live out its ministry in society ceases to be a body and becomes a ghostly shadow. A minister, or church member, who does not live out his faith and calling in the world is amputated from the body of Christ in effectiveness.

There are tensions as we live in the world. We are still tainted by sinful human nature. It is easy to say we live in the midst of a people of unclean lips. It is more difficult to admit that we are also people of unclean lips. The genuineness of our ministry is dependent upon our making this admission.

Nearly every person has some potential for attaining adult maturity. This is not something that can be determined by age. Maturity means one has the ability to cope more successfully with life's problems, to be effective in making and carrying out plans, to have a deep awareness and appreciation of one's surroundings, and to expand one's resources for a fulfilled life. This is essential in the work of ministry.

An adult is able to extend himself beyond family and church. This involves the capacity to have meaningful personal relationships with others of all ages and both sexes. Maturity implies moving away from casual and quickly dropped interests that are pursued for ulterior motives. Maturity comes as we extend ourselves into activities and interests where the reward comes from doing something for its own sake.

We must be able to welcome discipline. We have to know how to adapt to change.

The extension of oneself is both a danger and a challenge to the young minister at the beginning of his ministry. The danger lies in having a fantasy about the role of a minister that is logical but not rational. You can become so absorbed in "doing" ministry that you cease to "be" a minister. How do you minister to the human soul? If we are not careful, the soul becomes an object that we try to manipulate in ways that will fulfill our concept of the minister's role. Your ministry must be to persons in such a way that they get in touch with their own soul.

The challenge to the young minister is looking ahead to many years in which to grow. Learning to be a minister does not stop with the receiving of a degree. Most of what we learn is in the crucible of human experience. We need to extend ourselves beyond our fantasies of role and simply be persons who need to be ministered unto as much as we need to minister to others.

The adult is able to relate warmly to others. This requires both intimacy with and compassion toward others. An adult is ready for intimacy, which means both committing oneself to personal relationships and having the motivation to maintain them.

To be mature requires emotional security. An important quality of emotional security is self-acceptance. This means you acknowledge yourself as you are and as you were created to become. Mature people can accept the fact that they cannot be perfect in all respects. Yet, they strive toward the fulfillment of their potential.

Another important element in emotional security is an ability to function under stress. To be able to manage one's frustrations and still be able to function day to day is a difficult task, but necessary in growing toward maturity.

Emotional security is also dependent upon confidence in one's self expression. This is crucial for a church musician. To perform is to express oneself musically. It is easy to conclude that people do not like us if they do not like the way we sing, play, or conduct.

A mature person is in touch with reality, without distorting life to meet his own needs and purposes. All of us respond to the complexities of life with coping or defense mechanisms. However, overusing – or misusing – these mechanisms leads to a distortion of reality and to a misinterpretation of one's world. A mature mind is able to perceive the world correctly, in spite of necessary defense mechanisms.

The mature person has self-knowledge, which is insight into oneself. This means knowing what we can do, what we cannot do, what we ought to do, and the differences between them. Mature persons are able to make decisions and to act upon them responsibly when they have this self-knowledge.

The mature Christian has a faith system that provides life with a purpose, ideals, goals, and values. This kind of faith is what gives meaning to the life of a believer.

YOU ARE A MINISTER

What you have read so far are traits necessary if you want to lead in a ministry of music and worship. You must be a minister who has a calling *and* a ministry. Being a minister must be based upon who you are as a person and as a believer. You can learn a "bag of tricks" that will enable you to fill the role of a minister, but without a spiritual dimension you cannot *be* a minister.

A CALLING

One entering any form of ministry must have a sense of being called by God. This calling is expressed in three ways. First, there is the inner conviction that God's will for the person is to be in full-time ministry and the commitment of life to God. Second, there is the outer commitment to God's will by publicly declaring one's inner conviction and commitment. Third, there is the call of a church for one to serve as minister. No call is complete until it finds expression in these three ways.

A MINISTRY

What is ministry? This is a word that is bandied around a lot. Every Christian rock group, every Christian soloist, and every worship leader has a "ministry". But what is ministry? In the Hebrew Old Testament two words have been translated "ministry" in some Bibles. One word is *shareth* which means "serve" and is used in connection with the Levites carrying out their duties in the tabernacle and Temple. The other word is *'abodah* which means "work". This is used to describe any kind of work including the official duties of priests.

Three words are used in the New Testament that have been translated "ministry". One word is *diakonia*. This word appears in various forms and means "service" and "servant". Literally, this describes someone walking in the dust, or someone waiting tables. This is the word used to describe the "deacon". Another word is *leitourgia*. This word has several forms and means carrying out official duties. In

Hebrews chapters 8 and 9 it is used to describe the work of the priests in the Old Testament. A third New Testament word is *latreia*. This, too, is used to describe official duties being carried out.

The biblical languages give us no basis for describing ministry the way many people are describing it today. To be a minister is to be a servant. Ministry is to attend to the wants and needs of others. I define ministry as "meeting the needs of others in the name of Jesus." Anything less than this is not ministry.

How is the touring Christian rock band meeting the needs of others in the name of Jesus? Or is the rock band merely a group of Christians who give us concerts? How is your choir meeting the needs of others in the name of Jesus? Or is your choir a group giving Sunday morning concerts? How does a concert meet the needs of people in the name of Jesus? How are you personally meeting the needs of others in the name of Jesus? I believe we flippantly use ministry to justify what we are doing and getting recognition. What you and the choir and the rock band are doing may be Christian, but is it meeting the needs of others in the name of Jesus? How can you demonstrate that you are meeting people's needs in Jesus' name?

Using this definition, what is a minister? A minister is a person who meets the needs of others in the name of Jesus. Ministry in this sense is the ministry of the church itself, because everyone who is part of a church is meant to be a minister. This is not an exclusively New Testament idea. God told Moses to tell the Israelites, "You will be my holy nation and serve me as priests." The New Testament picks this idea up in 1 Peter 2:9: "But you are God's chosen and special people. You are a group of royal priests and a holy nation."

Without this understanding of ministry, the biblical figure of the church being the body of Christ has no meaning. The perfect church is a church that ministers, meeting the needs of people in the name of Jesus. It is the responsibility of every church member to be a minister, to meet the needs of people in the name of Jesus. This idea of ministry means the church is a living society through which the living Lord expresses Himself.

Though all the Israelites were priests, God commanded that special priests be selected from the tribe of Levi (Numbers 1:49-51; 3:5-13) to serve first in the tabernacle and then in the Temple. Though all Christians are to be ministers, God calls people to a specialized ministry and gives spiritual gifts to those people that will enable them to their specialized ministry. Consequently, anyone entering the specialized ministry as a leader of worship must give evidence that they have the gifts for that ministry.

This is why a church needs to issue a call to persons to serve in specialized ministries. The leader of worship is not a casual song leader who makes a living from the church as a professional musician. You are a minister of the church, who is declaring the message of the church through music on behalf of the church and with the support of the church. You are a helping-meet-the-needs-of-others-facilitator. You meet the needs of people in the church by helping them learn how to carry out their ministry, helping them to discover and use their gifts to meet the needs of others.

Whether you are actually called a "minister" or whether you are ordained is irrelevant. What matters is your conviction that you are acting for the church and with the church behind you as you meet the needs of people in the name of Jesus, whether these people are in the church or in the community. You are the person who in some way or other is the musical voice of the church. You are the person approved and set apart by the church to do on behalf of the church the work for which the church recognizes your spiritual gift.

According to Ephesians 4:11-12, your ministry is to enable church members to meet the needs of others through music. Music is not in those verses, but the task of the minister is: "to prepare all God's people for the work of Christian service" (v. 12, GNT). You are to proclaim the gospel through song, scripture, prayer and personal witness. You are responsible for the pastoral care and oversight of those under your charge. You are to lead others to reach their fullest Christian potential and to lead them to meet the needs of others in the name of Jesus. There is only one ministry: the ministry of Christ given to all believers through His church,

GIFT OR TALENT?

All Christians have at least one spiritual gift, but many have never developed that gift. A mature person recognizes his gift or gifts and develops the skills and competencies necessary to exercise his gift.

It has often been asked: What is the distinction between a gift and a talent? This is an important question for musicians since our art requires a great deal of natural talent. A spiritual gift is spiritual energy received from the Holy Spirit, energy that enables you to become a channel through which God's Spirit can flow out to other people. This might be in the form of an ability that you did not have prior to conversion. You were given the ability or gift as a result of your conversion. Or you may have received a special empowerment of a natural talent as a result of your conversion.

I need to continue to thirst for the knowledge.
enjoy friendships to cherish for future references.

The essential ingredient is your commitment to the Lord. I felt God's call to full-time Christian vocation when I was 16. In those days you had little choice for ministry; either be a pastor or a missionary, or the wife of a pastor or missionary. Very few churches had ministers of music or worship leaders. I asked my pastor to what job I should devote myself. He very wisely told me that my commitment was to Christ, not a job. What I did to fulfill my call would take care of itself if I were open to Christ's leadership. That has proven to be sound advice.

YOU NEED PREPARATION

One of the heresies current among Christians is the heresy that you don't have to be well trained to serve God. Another heresy is that Christian musicians do not have to be as well trained as secular musicians. Some people seem to think that the only thing you need to be a successful worship leader is a big smile and the ability to get along with people. If you just happen to have some musical skills that is an asset, but it is not really necessary. As with all heresies, these two are false.

There is no substitute for preparation. You need to be as well trained as your secular counterpart if not better trained. God deserves the best we can give him. If you are to function effectively as a worship leader you need to be prepared as fully as possible in music. You also need a philosophy and a theology of worship leadership.

MUSIC SKILLS

You need basic music theory skills. You need to be able to recognize what harmony the choir should be singing or the instruments to be playing to ensure they are in tune. You need to know how instruments transpose and to write out parts for them to play. You need to know the harmonic styles of different periods of music so you will perform pieces properly. You need to be able to harmonize simple melodies.

You need skills in conducting. I knew a worship leader who said he could not direct the Pastoral Symphony from Handel's "Messiah" because it had no words. That demonstrated a real weakness in conducting skill. You need to know how to conduct voices, instruments and children. You need to know how to lead congregational singing. You need to know how to plan an efficient and effective rehearsal.

— seek for help and never feel weak.

Good communication with congregation.

The worship leader has teaching as a primary task in ministry. You cannot teach something you have never learned. You cannot teach effectively unless you know how people learn and how you can guide that learning. The learning tasks of the worship leader are to help each church member to develop music skills, attitudes and appreciations, and knowledge. Education for music means to help people develop the skills and techniques of music leadership. Education through music means to use music as a tool for reaching nonmusical ends in the church.

Another aspect of the worship leader's ministry is performing. Whether doing solos or conducting, you must be able to communicate effectively at a high level of musical performance. Just as the pastor studies biblical languages, biblical exegesis, and sermon building to become an effective performer through preaching, worship leaders study music theory, music history, and have private instruction in a performing area that enables them to perform effectively through music.

Any weakness you have in leading a choir or a praise band will limit your effectiveness in ministry. If you cannot train others in music and worship skills, your effectiveness is limited. If you cannot train others to become music leaders your effectiveness is limited.

Body language?

A Philosophy of Worship Leadership

By philosophy I mean practical thinking about your work. What is your purpose, your reason for ministry as a worship leader in your church? What are your personal goals and values for ministry? What goals, values and tasks do you envision for the ministry that is your responsibility? Answers to these questions will give you a mission statement for yourself and your ministry.

A mission statement provides clarity and gives you a sense of purpose both for yourself and for the organization of your work. A mission statement defines who you are, what your ministry is, how you will live and how you will do your work. You should try to develop a personal mission statement for your own guidance and an organizational mission statement for your ministry. You need a personal mission statement, a mission statement for the ministry you provide and a mission statement for each segment of your ministry. For example, what is the purpose of an adult choir? What is the purpose of children's choirs? A praise team? A praise band? If you cannot make a mission statement for these groups, why do you have them?

In the sample mission statements that follow, notice the emphasis upon meeting the needs of others. First, here is a mission statement that might help you to develop your own personal mission statement:

I love to learn!

> **EXAMPLE:** *Personal Mission Statement*
>
> "My purpose is to serve both God and First Community Church to the fullest extent possible. I will declare the message of the church through music and worship, on behalf of the church. Through my ministry I will help others to discover, develop, and use their God-given gifts in all aspects of music. I will prepare myself and the congregation for a deeper encounter with God in spirit and in truth each Sunday."

Here is a ministry mission statement that might help you to develop a mission statement for your total ministry:

> **EXAMPLE:** *Ministry Mission Statement*
>
> The mission of the music and worship ministry of First Community Church is to provide opportunities for:
>
> • A deeper experience of God in spirit and in truth for the membership through worship.
>
> • People to use their gifts in meeting the needs of others through making music and leading worship.
>
> • People to do the work of Christ through music organizations.
>
> • Members of music organizations to receive pastoral care.
>
> • Those who are responsible for music and worship leadership to receive training for their tasks.
>
> • The church membership to receive training in music and worship.

A THEOLOGY OF WORSHIP LEADERSHIP

If you are going to be a worship leader, you need a depth of biblical knowledge and theological insight. What do the Scriptures say about worship leadership? What principles are found in the Bible that can give guidance to you? What is the nature of the church? How is the church supposed to function? These are questions you need to have firm answers for.

Then you need to be able to bring theology and Scripture to bear upon the worship resources you select. You must have insight into music and how it functions in worship. Somehow your theological, biblical and musical selves need to be brought together. You will be dealing constantly with criteria for choosing and evaluating the things you include in worship.

HOPE AND HELP

As you can see, any weakness in any of these areas will diminish your effectiveness as a leader. So, what do you do if you don't have these skills? There is both hope and help.

First, there is hope. You can develop these skills. Not everyone can attain a high level of proficiency in all areas of music, but you can attain sufficient proficiency to be an effective worship leader. There is hope for you if you really want to be an effective leader.

Second, there is help from many different sources. A college or university near you may offer music and Bible courses you could take. There are many correspondence courses available both from colleges and universities as well as Alexander University (www.alexanderpublishing.com) that can help you gain skills in music theory and instrumentation. Other correspondence courses are available in Bible and theology. There are numerous one to three day workshops and conferences that provide training in all these subjects. Then, you can learn by reading the many books that are available.

Call for help on particular situations.

Talk to other worship leaders who have these skills. Ask them for books to read. Ask them if they will mentor you. Above all, pray that God will make you the worship leader He wants you to be!

we are not gone. know how to ask and study.

CHAPTER SUMMARY

In this chapter we have thought about you as a person and some of the issues to be pursued in later chapters.

- You are a person who is an emotional creature, a social creature, and with the potentiality of becoming an adult in full maturity.

- You are a Christian, one committed in faith to Jesus Christ.

- To minister is to meet the needs of others in the name of Jesus.

- You are called of God to the specialized ministry of worship leadership.

- You are a minister of the church, and you declare the message of the church through music on behalf of the church and with the support of the church.

- You have a ministry of proclamation, pastoral care, and leadership.

- You are to enable others to do the work of Christ.

- You need preparation in music, and you need a philosophy and a theology of worship leadership.

Do I accept change very well? embrace it.
we have to be able to accept it. embrace it.

CHAPTER 2

YOU AND YOUR MUSIC

The average worship leader works with music daily, but perhaps has never stopped to consider what you are working with. It is not that you do not know what music is, but that you have had little opportunity to put all of this theoretical knowledge into a unified whole. In this chapter we shall look at music as sound, as form, as expression, and as symbol.

MUSIC AS SOUND

As a field of study, music is the result of thought. It is a conceptual system that deals with the relationship of musical sounds to one another. These concepts are more than ideas. When music is performed we are hearing musical concepts that have been organized into patterns of sound, and the musical composition is what a composer has thought to be the best way to organize sound.

While all cultures seem to have some kind of music, there is no one universal sound that can be defined as music. Different cultures have different ideas about how sound should be organized and what kinds of sounds can be formed into a composition. This is why music of non-Western cultures sounds different to us. What makes sound into music is determined by a culture and not by any preexistent, eternal rules that man discovers.

Each period of Western music history has contained many different rules for writing and performing music. Composers have written music in a certain way, and when a large body of music thus composed has been produced, it is then possible to analyze that music and to discover what rules were consciously or unconsciously at work in the mind of the composer.

Once rules have been discovered for composing music, a tradition is established which other composers may or may not follow as they write music. History has shown that a music tradition has not existed very long before new composers begin to challenge that tradition and to write music in new and different ways. Often, this has led to arguments between two or more groups of composers and their followers over the correct rules to follow in composing music.

Music comes before the rules. Understanding how sound is made into music requires a knowledge of the historical and cultural context in which it has been written. Our understanding of music also requires the knowledge of certain terms that are used to describe musical sounds. For example, a chorale motet is a term that describes a particular type of organized musical sound.

Music is sound [and silence] that is organized in time. Given this definition almost any sound could become a musical sound. Regular musical instruments can make music as well as things we would not consider to be musical instruments. For example, one 20th century composition I know of requires four vacuum sweepers in addition to a symphony orchestra! Composers take sound and do all kind of things with it in order to make music.

You can identify sounds by using adjectives, such as short/long, slow/fast, high/low, sad/happy, sharp/dull, muffled/bright, etc. Rarely will a piece of music contain only one kind of sound; that would be uninteresting. Generally music will use many different kinds of sound.

If sounds are to make sense to us they have to be organized in some fashion. One long continuous sound would not be very interesting, so composers organize sounds that are higher and lower, longer and shorter, faster and slower, etc. Three elements of sound combine to make what we call music: rhythm, pitch and timbre.

RHYTHM

Rhythm is the element that gives us a sense that the music is "moving." Rhythm is made up of five things: beat, duration, accent, tempo and meter.

Pulse or beat is the thing that holds music together. You have a heartbeat which is your pulse. Most people have a normal heartbeat of 70-80 beats per minute. The beat is faster after exercise and slower when we sleep. The beat in music can move slowly, fast and in between. A beat can be prominent or non-prominent.

Duration is how long a sound or silence lasts. Some sounds and silences are short; others are long. Beats are grouped in sets, the most common sets being in 2's, 3's and 4's.

Accent is the stress put upon certain beats. Beats are grouped in 2, 3, 4, etc. Generally the first beat of a set is given more stress or accent than other notes in the measure.

Tempo is the term used to describe the speed of the beat. When the beat of music is about the same as your own pulse the music has a moderate tempo. If the music beat is faster than your normal heart rate the tempo is fast. If the beat of music is slower than your normal heart rate the tempo is slow.

Meter is the grouping of beats in two's, three's and combinations. Sometimes the meter grouping is steady but the melody does not seem to fit the beat pattern. This is called syncopation. The meter organization is determined by strong and weak accents.

PITCH

Pitch in music refers to the lows and highs of music sounds. Pitch has three elements: melody, tonality and harmony.

A *melody* is a coherent succession of pitches that has shape and rhythm and implies harmony. Melodies may be prominent or non-prominent. The melodic idea may be long or short and may be ornamented with extra notes. A melody may have repetition of a phrase or a melodic idea that is heard again. A melody may have the repetition of a melodic idea or portion of a melodic idea in another part. A melody may have an immediate repetition of a melodic idea in the same voice using different pitches.

This is a gross oversimplification, but *tonality* is the arrangement of all the tones and chords of a composition in relation to the first note of a scale. This is what a key, such as the key of C, means: all the tones and chords are written in relation to the note C which is the first note of the C scale.

Some sounds can be heard by themselves, but at other times several sounds will be combined and can be heard simultaneously. *Harmony* is the term used to describe two or more sounds heard simultaneously.

TIMBRE

Timbre is the specific quality of sound produced by an instrument, voice or sound-generating device in musical performance. For example, in choirs, a soprano sounds different than a bass. In orchestras, a cello sounds different than a flute.

MUSIC AS FORM

Any kind of form refers to how something appears to us. We think of the form of a house or the form of a tree. Music as sound appears to us in three ways: the form of sound, the form of structure, and the form of mood or expression.

NATURAL FORM

The natural form of music is sound before it has been organized or controlled. This means any sound could become music. Sound is the raw material out of which music is created. Prior to this century, only certain kinds of sound were considered to be true musical sounds in Western music. Today, composers use all kinds of sounds to produce music. Not only are traditional musical instruments used to produce sound, but many other things as well.

STRUCTURAL FORM

The composer takes the raw material of sound and does something with it and to it. Structural form is the way sound is organized into music. Music structure includes traditional forms such as rondo, etc., as well as the basic elements of harmony, rhythm, melody, and counterpoint. The perception of structural form requires us to discern four elements that make up structure: proportion, balance, sequence and rhythmic flow, transition and emphasis, and stress or accent.

Proportion is what enables us to compare the different parts of a composition. We can compare the proportion of melody to harmony, of counterpoint to homophony, of one tempo change to another, etc.

Balance is achieved by repeating melodies, rhythms, motifs, and other elements at various places in a piece of music in alternation with other contrasting elements. The traditional terms for musical form are merely labels that describe how a composer balances the various parts of his composition.

Composers are limited in the ways they can achieve balance only by their creative genius. Some methods of achieving balance are more recognizable than others. Some of the resistance to contemporary music is due to the difficulty some have in perceiving any musical balance.

Sequence and rhythmic flow are terms that describe the order of musical events. Sequence refers to what order the sounds follow, such as which chords follow other chords and what notes of a melody follow other notes. Rhythm refers to the flow or motion of sound. This includes tempo, meter, pulse, duration of pitches and silences, dynamics, timbre, phrases, and periods.

Transition and emphasis are terms that describe changes in the music. A composition changes from one mood to another and from one speed to another, giving us the impression of motion and change. We can stop music, speed it up, slow it down, and have the sensation of movement through time. These changes are transition, and their importance in the composition is emphasis.

Stress or accent is the extra emphasis placed upon certain notes, phrases, or pulses. Stress is obvious in spoken language and in singing, since the proper articulation of language requires an additional stress or accent to be placed on certain syllables or words. This same stress or accent is necessary for the articulation of music.

EXPRESSIVE FORM

Sound produces a response both in humans and in animals that can be called "mood." Mood is a response to sound similar to a reflex action of an arm or a leg, or the human response to other types of stimuli. When we use words to describe the mood produced by music, we are referring to the expressive form of music. The frequency of sound (high–low), its speed (tempo), its pleasantness or unpleasantness (consonance–dissonance), and its intensity (loud–soft) are a few of the many ways we describe the mood produced by music.

In addition, the composer uses words and phrases that are written on the score by which he tries to convey the general mood of his music to the performer. Traditionally, composers have used Italian words since musicians understand these universally. However, more and more composers are now using words and phrases in their own language instead.

Any words or phrases we might use to describe the mood of music are not determined by the structure of the sounds and are not necessarily an integral part of those sounds. We use words and phrases that describe our reactions to the music and we might use words the composer would never think of using.

MUSIC AS EXPRESSION

The most obvious effect of music is the response it elicits from the listener. We respond to music because it expresses something for us, and we can express ourselves through the music. "To express" means to "put into words." If we think of music as expression, we need to think about how we can put it into words.

STYLE

Style in music is like style in clothing or hair or cars or anything else. It is the way composers at a specific time write music in a particular way. From your own experience you can tell the difference between rap, rock-and-roll, and country-western music. That difference is style.

Style in music is that which makes a piece of music distinctive of a composer, a place, or a time. Style is the particular way sound is organized and structured. The composer organizes his sound according to his own personality, training, and the historical period in which he lives. A composer's style cannot be discovered only in one piece of music, but through the performance and analysis of many of his works. When the composer writes many pieces of music and consistently uses particular rhythms, harmonies, types of melodies, etc., we can describe his style in terms of the techniques he has employed. When several composers within the same historical period write music in a similar way, we then classify music according to Romantic style or Classic style, etc.

For the conductor and performer, the elements of style are structural devices that help him know how the music should be performed. In addition, the performer or conductor uses his knowledge of music history to recreate as nearly as possible the music as originally intended.

However, we can distinguish some nonmusical elements of style that are related to what the composer is as a person. For example, the ideas behind music in the Classical period were that music should be kept simple without obscuring melody and harmony with decoration, counterpoint, or similar devices. In Impressionism, the idea was for objective reality to be distorted in such a way that details are lacking and only an impression remains. The music of Debussy and Ravel are examples of this, for they did not try to imitate sounds of nature or to give musical descriptions, but to create the emotions produced by sounds of nature, events, and situations.

In church music, these nonmusical elements of style have been used to create music that is "holy" and produced certain religious feelings, or that supposedly produced some kind of communion with the divine. It is important that worship leaders understand the nonmusical ideas that have influenced a composition, for this gives understanding about the intentions of the composer apart from the notes written on the score.

The composer takes sound, the natural form of music, and shapes it into different structures. But what is expressed in the structure? Our conclusion is:

the underlying subject matter of music is an expression of the ultimate concern both of the composer and the listener. A composition exists as a cultural creation in its own right. It embodies the value system of the composer. However, when a person encounters that composition, he relates to it according to his own value system.

How Music Expresses

For the use of music in worship, what music expresses is dependent entirely upon the person who is listening to it. Some people would describe their responses to music in terms of liking a melody, or feeling a strong rhythm, or even in more complex descriptions.

Others would describe music in terms of how the music makes them feel, such as "happy," "near to God," "elation," or some other feeling. Fewer people would perhaps attempt to describe their responses to music in terms of their inner feelings, since the meaning of music to them lies in their ability to experience the inner feelings through music without describing or talking about it.

The value and significance of music to an individual will depend upon his ability to describe his responses in some way. If he is inclined to describe his responses only in terms of a nonmusical scene, event, or story, he will probably not "like" music that does not offer this opportunity for imagery. The ability of people to respond to many types of music could be increased by their attempting to describe those responses in many different ways through familiarity with many different types of music.

Man responds to the stimuli of sound biologically, both to the way sound is organized and the mental images sound stimuli produce. We perceive music the way we perceive any other part of the objective world. Sound produces a general response both in humans and animals that is a mood.

As people listen to music, they should be free to find their own expression in, and through music. Yet church members can be guided into various ways of finding expression in and through music. Just as one can be guided into a greater linguistic expression through the acquisition and use of a larger language vocabulary, one can be guided into a greater musical expression through the acquisition and use of a larger musical vocabulary and the exposure to many kinds of music.

We should be able to describe some of our responses in religious terms if we are to have a religious expression in and through music. The most immediate descriptions would be of religious feelings aroused in us by music. However, it is possible that the inner emotional life could find proper religious expression as well through music.

Music as Symbol

One of the distinctions between people and animals is the human ability to produce symbols. The infant soon realizes that there is a world existing outside himself to which he must relate. As the child grows and experiences his world, he learns to give names to things and to others and to describe how he feels and thinks. This is the process of making symbols, for language is the most obvious and basic form of symbolism. In a language, certain sounds and words express ideas, objects, feelings, and experiences. Sounds and combinations of letters become associated with reality over a long period of time. Without this association, lingual communication would be impossible. Man cannot think without some kind of language, and language is determined by usage and not by an arbitrary decree.

Any language derives its existence and meaning through human experience. One is not born with a ready-made language as part of his brain cells. He is born with the capacity for making a language that arises within him as he becomes involved with the world around him.

Language is not the only kind of symbol; there are also nonlinguistic symbols. Generally, symbols are divided into discursive and non-discursive groups. Discursive symbols are linguistic symbols used to describe human experience verbally. Non-discursive symbols are nonverbal and describe human experience and feeling through gestures, art objects, etc. Some symbols may combine some elements of both the discursive and non-discursive types.

We can make a further division of symbols into groups such as artistic symbols, religious symbols, cultural symbols, and similar types. We can see, then, that the worship leader must work with both discursive and non-discursive symbols that are religious, cultural, and artistic. Religious symbols (such as God, faith, salvation) are verbal or discursive in nature. Music as an artistic symbol is nonverbal or non-discursive. When we have words associated with music we have both discursive and non-discursive symbols, but the non-discursive elements probably predominate.

The Origin of Religious Symbols

All symbols, regardless of their classification, are born out of man's experience of living. Religious symbols are born out of man's encounter with events over which he has no control. Philosophers use the term "The Unconditioned" to describe these situations and events. Man is unable to dictate the conditions of relationship between himself and certain aspects of his existence. For example, while man may be able to dictate the manner in which he dies, he has no control over the fact that he will die. Death is part of The Unconditioned.

In the face of The Unconditioned, man has sought to discover what relationship must exist if he is to make peace with the unconditioned elements of life. Out of this search have grown various religious beliefs and practices that relate man to some kind of deity.

The symbols that are born out of this encounter with The Unconditioned are religious symbols, though they may not be Christian symbols. As Christians, we can refer to God as "Father" because we have both a concept of and an experience of fatherhood in human relationships and we have experienced God in this relationship. One's concept of religion is greatly influenced by his use of and understanding of symbols such as "father," "love," "trust," and similar terms. When a word like father expresses, communicates, and reveals the relationship between God and man, father becomes a religious symbol.

THE ORIGIN OF THE MUSIC SYMBOL

No one knows with any certainty why we have music. Various reasons have been given, such as:

1. We are searching for pleasure through music;

2. We have a natural desire for beauty that can be found in music;

3. We need to contemplate something beyond ourselves and music is an object of contemplation and an accompaniment to the act of contemplation;

4. We have a biological need for the sensory stimuli of music;

5. We need to express qualities of our inner selves in a way that words alone cannot express.

All of these viewpoints have their merits, and no one of them is completely wrong. However, we can raise questions about them, such as: What kind of pleasure are we seeking through music? What is beauty? How do we respond to music biologically? How is music an object for contemplation? What is the nature of the inner life we are trying to express through music?

Perhaps the most satisfactory reason for having music is as a symbol of time. We cannot control time, though we can control various elements of time. Time is part of The Unconditioned; we cannot control time. There are two kinds of time: clock time, which is ongoing and strictly measured; and eternal time, which is in the realm of timelessness in terms of its being strictly measured. These two types of time are found in the New Testament. *Chronos* is clock time and *kairos* is eternal time. Eternal time is reflected in this familiar passage: "For while we were still helpless, at the right time [*kairos*] Christ died for the ungodly." (Romans 5:6, NASB).

Music occurs both in clock time and eternal time. Recurring beats, rhythmic patterns, melodies, and other musical elements are clock time. But we can change clock time by slowing it down or speeding it up. Few musicians appreciate the importance of silence in music, for in this way time is brought to a halt. However, underneath this clock time is a sense of eternal time. When music comes to a rest or a long pause, we still have the sense of motion, the music moving toward some distant end.

Music becomes a symbol for ideal time, eternal time, a time we would like to have if we could control it or experience it completely. Music for the church should be very much in "time and eternity" and help us to relate ourselves to eternal life.

THE FUNCTION OF THE MUSIC SYMBOL

Symbols participate in reality, communicate reality, reveal reality and represent reality. As an artistic symbol, music functions like all other symbols.

- Music participates in reality. Music is a part of reality as sound; a cultural art form; a particular and individual cultural creation of a composer; an artistic reality; and an artistic expression of relationship to The Unconditioned.

- Music communicates the concepts of the composer for organizing sound; the concepts of a culture that defines what kinds of sounds are musical sounds; the sensitivity of a person to musical stimuli; the responses elicited from us by music; and qualities of The Unconditioned.

- Music reveals reality. Music is revelatory when the term "music" becomes understood through musical experience; when we discover that music expresses something both for us and to us; and when music opens up new levels of reality both within us and in the objective world.

- Music is representative both of a cultural reality and a personal reality when the term "music" is equivalent to the sum total of our musical sensitivity and taste; our musical responses; and the things expressed through music.

MUSIC AS A LITURGICAL SYMBOL

As Christians, we give a religious interpretation of the world and everything in it. This interpretation is not just a religious one, but a particular religious interpretation based upon the Scriptures, Christian experience, and the history of Christianity. Contemporary theologians are inclined toward the position that everyone and every interpretation is religious. This conclusion is based upon the fact that all persons are confronted with The Unconditioned and must relate to it in some way. When a relationship has been established between a person and the unconditioned elements of life, this is a religious relationship, but not necessarily a Christian relationship.

For the Christian God is more than The Unconditioned. He is the eternal, holy, and loving God who has been revealed through Jesus Christ. Christians have discovered both linguistic and nonlinguistic symbols that not only enable them to communicate their relationship to God, but which also reveal God to them and enable them to express their relationship to God. Church music is one way in which Christians both describe and experience the life of the Holy Spirit who helps them to rise above human finitude and the unconditioned elements of life.

God and the other realities of the Christian faith can be perceived in many ways other than in language or linguistic symbols: through gestures, through physical objects (such as the Bible and the cross), and through specific acts (such as baptism and the Lord's Supper).

A liturgical symbol is any gesture, object, act, or art form that can participate with linguistic symbols to communicate, reveal, and represent Christian faith. The word liturgical is used because liturgy is a word associated with the life of the church. Liturgy is derived from the Greek word *leiturgos,* the same word from which we get the word *laity.* In the Christian context, *leiturgos* means the total life of the individual believer and his participation in the Body of Christ. A liturgical symbol is anything found in reality that can function in the corporate and individual life of the body of Christ.

We must exercise care in giving the liturgical symbol label to every piece of music that is called "church music." Music has the potential of becoming a liturgical symbol only when all of reality is viewed from the Christian perspective. If we see the world and everything in it as the handiwork of God that He has given to man for care and development through man's stewardship, then music can symbolize this world view.

When music can function in the life of the body of Christ, then it becomes a liturgical symbol. Within this context, nearly any kind of music could become a liturgical symbol. The ability of any musical composition to become such a symbol is dependent upon the Christian experience of the person and the manner in which this experience is expressed in linguistic religious symbols; the degree to which a person can perceive and respond to different kinds of music; and God choosing to reveal Himself more fully through a piece of music, thereby imbuing the music with spiritual power.

Much of the conflict over music and worship styles is based upon what music symbolizes to different people. For many people older and traditional forms of music symbolize and embody their religious experience. These forms of music do not symbolize the religious experience of those who prefer contemporary popular music in the church.

If we are to relate music to worship in a meaningful way, it is necessary to understand music as a potential liturgical symbol. We cannot arbitrarily produce music that will function as a liturgical symbol; it must be born out of religious and musical experiences. If the experiences that produce the symbol cease to exist, the symbol dies. Hence, we can neither select certain music to become a liturgical symbol nor retain music already well used in the belief that it is a valid liturgical symbol.

Worship leadership in churches must be aware of the religious experiences of their members, how these experiences are growing, how these religious experiences are expressed linguistically, and the level of musical sensitivity and taste within the church. They must then provide musical experiences that will increase the musical understanding and expression of everyone in the congregation.

SUMMARY

1. Music is organized and controlled sound moving in time. Pitch, duration, rhythm, and tempo are terms which describe how sound is organized and controlled.

2. Music appears to us as form. There is natural form, or sound before it has been organized and controlled; structural form, or the way sounds are organized; and expressive form, or the mood produced by music.

3. Music is expression. We can put our responses to music into words, which may be either words that describe the music or words that describe our feelings aroused by the music.

4. Music is a symbol that participates in, communicates, reveals, and represents reality. As an artistic symbol, music is a non-discursive symbol of the inner life of man.

CHAPTER 3

You And Your Philosophy

The worship leader needs a philosophy of church music. This philosophy can be defined as a way of thinking reflectively about certain problems, beliefs, and attitudes toward church music. He or she needs to think about church music, reflectively in the manner of a philosopher. The end result of this thinking will be a philosophy of church music that includes values, understandings, attitudes, convictions, ideals, and basic concepts about church music and its function in the church.

Any philosophy is influenced by contributions from other fields of knowledge. A philosopher approaches his task from his basic presuppositions about life, people, God, and anything else that makes him the person he is. Before one is a philosopher he is a human being with everything that has contributed to his humanity. The evangelical worship leader must think reflectively about music within the framework of a Christian belief system.

Problems in Formulating a Philosophy

Thinking reflectively about church music in hopes of formulating a systematic philosophy is difficult, for there are at least three problems that must be dealt with. First, there is the problem of relating one's theological convictions to one's gifts and training in music. It may seem that the two are so far apart there is no need to even bother with an attempt to relate them. Yet the worship leader needs help in communicating with non-Christian musicians about music and its place in the church and why church music has been chosen as a field of service.

Second, traditional theological studies do not equip the musician with ways of evaluating music as music. One may learn how music functions in worship and evangelism and how music is related to the life and work of the church, but the study of theology does not equip one to determine if this piece of music is better than another.

27

Third, the average church congregation has not given serious thought to the use and purposes of church music. Thus, few churches have developed a philosophy that can help them plan a music program. There may be little or no reflective thinking about music in the church over the long term due to the wishes of pastor or congregation, or the week–to–week demands of providing music for worship services. What is "good" and usable music is based upon current standards and values rather than a commonly accepted philosophy of music that gives direction to the church.

PROBLEMS OF THEOLOGY

If the worship leader is to think reflectively within the framework of theological beliefs, these questions must be raised:

- Can music reveal God and/or religious truths?
- Must music be associated with worship in order to be sacred?
- Is there anything about the sounds of music that determines if it is sacred or secular?
- Is music without a text as appropriate for religious purposes as music with a text?

Answering these questions requires some serious theological thought, for one must define what "God" and "religious truth" and the other terms mean. Such definitions require more than an intellectual agreement with a creed or statement of faith.

Coming to grips with one's own personal theology can often be a knotty experience. Even more difficult is the attempt to reconcile one's theology with the ideals of professional musicianship. In the non-Christian musical world there is no point of reference for the creative output of men other than themselves. At one time in history the church was the point of reference and musicians devoted their attention to distinctively Christian creations. The needs and demands of a church for its music may fall far short of secular standards of musicianship. The worship leader has the agonizing task of reconciling the two.

PROBLEMS OF DENOMINATIONALISM

The denominational heritage of the church musician may provide little help in thinking about church music reflectively. Musical taste may be determined largely by the wishes of a congregation or pastor. The church musician is subject to the worship patterns of his denomination, and the tensions and struggles experienced are part of the deep gulf that has separated faith and the arts over some four centuries.

In Protestant churches there have been few attempts to develop a music philosophy for an entire denomination similar to the formulation of creeds and/or statements of faith. Until such efforts are put forth, the church musician will remain confused and be subject to the whims of local pastors and congregations.

TENSIONS IN MUSICAL AESTHETICS

Many people are frightened by the word aesthetics because it seems to be a very confusing field of study. Generally, we tend to think of aesthetics as having something to do with "beauty." This is not the way we should think of aesthetics as worship leaders.

The word aesthetics comes from the Greek word *aisthetikos*, which means to gain knowledge through the senses. When you eat a green apple, your taste gives you the knowledge whether or not it is ripe. From the meaning of the original Greek word, eating a green apple is an aesthetic experience. We need to recapture this meaning for aesthetics today since all knowledge has some element of sense experience.

By way of contrast, the intellectual side of gaining knowledge is expressed by the Greek word *noetikos*, which means reasoning or reflection. Noetic thinking can occur without any sense experience external to the mind to stimulate thought.

All of our thinking has both aesthetic and noetic elements. Few of our thoughts would be completely one or the other, for most thinking lies somewhere in between. Some thought processes are more noetic, while other processes are more aesthetic. Theology is more noetic than music and music more aesthetic than theology, but both involve sense perception, feeling, reasoning, and reflection. Theology and music are two ways of looking at the same thing.

How did beauty get mixed up in all this? In Greek philosophy, something was beautiful when it fulfilled its purpose and/or design. Early in the nineteenth century German philosophers, imbued with the spirit of Romanticism, began to write about abstract beauty as an ideal. Today, we are not as concerned about beauty as we are about music being a kind of sense perception, the meaning of that perception, and its quality.

Striking a balance between these two ways of gaining knowledge creates tensions we need to recognize and learn to live with. Tensions are not bad in themselves and can be useful when used creatively, as when holding a bridge up.

FORM VS. EMOTION

There is tension between the emotional aspects of music and its structural aspects. This tension can be expressed in a question. Is a composition suitable for worship because of the way it has been written, or because of the religious emotion it creates within us?

A formalist is one who would put emphasis upon how music is written. He would say that meaning in music is determined by its technical aspects and not in any stories, scenes, ethical ideas, emotions, or moral uplift the music is supposed to be representing. The formalist would say, too, that music is suitable for worship when it is performed in a service, if the text bears some reference to God, and the title or the cover page designates the music as sacred.

An emotionalist would take the opposite view, saying that meaning in music is experienced in feelings of awe and reverence. Music is "spiritual" in its own right since it arouses these feelings in us. The emotionalist would make no distinction between sacred and secular music or music suitable for worship. Any music is suitable which produces awe and reverence. Experiencing the music is the same, or nearly the same, as experiencing God. Music is a source of religious knowledge since the experience of awe and reverence is the same as the experience of worship.

Since music appears to us both as expression and structure, this is a false division. The answer to the question of suitability is to consider both how the music is composed and what religious emotions can be created through the music. Seldom will we discover the perfect piece of music where both the technical and emotional aspects are balanced. Few musicians would agree to any list of examples drawn up by another musician. Suitability falls back upon the individual and his sensitivity and taste.

TOOL VS. ART

Is church music merely a tool we use to reach religious ends, or is church music really an art form? As seen above, the formalist would say church music is an art form and the emotionalist would tend to say church music is a tool we use.

From birth to death, our thinking and learning is a process of discovering the objective world that exists apart from us. Not only do we discover our world; we place values on the things in our world. We place value upon what we discover in the world because there is a quality about objective reality that enables us to think about it. As we think, reality is organized mentally and emotionally into varying degrees of values. Those things that make our lives better qualitatively are what we value most highly.

Music is a part of objective reality that the individual must discover. Each person determines the degree to which music makes life better. We do not know all the factors that go into making value judgments about music, but music does have a quality that enables us to think seriously about it.

Whether church music is merely a tool for religious ends or an art form can be determined only by asking some ultimate questions, such as: What is the value of this piece of music to me? Why do I value it? What would this music sound like if the melody went up rather than down? How did the composer create a feeling of tension and release? When such questions can be asked seriously about a composition, we are treating it as an art form. When we cannot ask such questions seriously, we are treating the music as a tool for nonmusical ends.

For music to be a tool rather than a great work of art is not bad, since it may give enjoyment and in this sense have value. Art philosophers have generally regarded the art forms of music as those compositions that can be analyzed and discussed repeatedly, with something new seeming to arise each time they are performed and analyzed.

At the same time, the individual listener may or may not agree with the critics and philosophers about the value of a particular composition. Most musicians would agree that Bach was a masterful composer and his work represents art, but not every musician likes Bach. So there remains the tension between a person's value judgments and what others say about the same composition.

Church music should be composed and performed as artistically as possible, and used as a tool to reach specific religious ends. This would require us to be open to all kinds of music and to use whatever kind of music we think is appropriate for the occasion. This would also require us to help people think about church music so they can make a valid value judgment about it.

In any single worship service there will be some people who perceive the music as something they can contemplate. Others will perceive the same music as a tool to accompany prayer, praise, and other religious responses. It is a question of whether the music is something to contemplate in its own right or a vehicle that leads us to greater religious devotion. In practice, we should present music in worship that provides both, if at all possible.

FREEDOM VS. RESPONSIBILITY

The tension between music as a tool and music as an art object leads us to the tension between freedom and responsibility. No one authority can impose value judgments about music upon a person. Value judgments must come from within the person. In order to make value judgments about music the person must be a self who is free to make those judgments. Freedom is not an isolated function of man, but is a part of man as a complete and rational self.

This tension can also be stated in a series of questions that must be answered: does the church composer write and perform music that communicates with the congregation, or does he or she compose and perform music of personal tastes and desires? How free is the church composer to create and to perform music apart from the congregation? Does the church composer have any responsibility as well as freedom? If so, is this a responsibility to himself, to God or to his congregation? Is it possible to compose freely and be responsible to self, God and the congregation at the same time?

Similarly, there are questions that must be raised and answered by each member of a church: Is a piece of music good or bad because I think so, or because my minister of music says so? Can I expect church musicians to communicate directly to me, or must I search for what they are trying to say through their music? Do I have a responsibility to church musicians?

CONCLUSION

We have raised more questions than answers in this discussion. That has been deliberate, for any answers will always be tentative and related to a specific church situation. These questions are of particular significance to the church musician, since the church demands intelligibility in its music. Many serious musicians are not writing or performing music for churches because they feel the church limits their freedom. Similarly, many church members are not accepting some types of church music because they feel it is irrelevant to their spiritual and musical needs.

A person becomes a complete person only when he or she can understand and shape reality according to values and meanings. We should strive for a balance between what the congregation wants and needs and what the musician wants and needs.

SUMMARY

1. A philosophy of church music is thinking reflectively about the problems, beliefs, and attitudes one has toward church music.

2. There are three problems in formulating a philosophy of church music: relating one's theology to one's music training and gifts; the absence of theological criteria for evaluating music as music; and the lack of serious thought about church music by the average congregation.

3. The problems for a philosophy of church music are those that require reflection about music; those that require serious theological thought; and those of denominational tradition and practice.

4. Aesthetics means to gain knowledge through the senses; and for music, this is primarily through the sense of hearing.

5. Some of the tensions in musical aesthetics are: form vs. emotion, tool vs. art and freedom vs. responsibility.

CHAPTER 4

YOU AND YOUR THEOLOGY

The fact that we think of "church" music and worship leaders implies there are theological considerations that must be taken into account. The worship leader must think about his or her work in the manner of a pastor, just as one must think like a philosopher. There may be some confusion on the part of some worship leaders due to a misunderstanding of what theology is and the equating of theology with doctrine. What is theology?

First, theology as a word comes from two Greek words: *theos,* meaning "god," and *logos,* meaning "word" or "rational thought." As a field of study, then, theology is supposedly rational thinking about a god. Theology is not peculiar just to the Christian religion, for Muslims and others also have a theology. Nor is theology limited to thinking about a god. Consequently, I will think in terms of Christian theology, which distinguishes our theology from other groups. Christian theology would include all of the presuppositions of the Christian faith studied in a rational way.

Second, theology is an attempt to answer various questions concerning some of the great issues of life, such as the nature of God or the nature and destiny of man. In this regard, there may be no clear line drawn between philosophy and theology, for philosophers raise some of the same questions raised by pastors. What differences exist would be in the answers given and where one goes to find the answers.

The philosopher would appeal more to nature and to human reason as sources for his answers. The pastor would appeal to divine revelation and the Bible as sources for his answers. However, the theologian needs to use human reason and philosophical language in order to raise questions and to communicate answers. Some contemporary theologians specialize in what is known as philosophic theology, asking philosophic questions and then giving theological answers.

Third, theology is the private personal expression of individual religious experience. As these expressions are related to those of others, a consensus of belief is made which become organized statements of doctrine. Doctrine is intended to be the norm by which religious beliefs and behavior are evaluated. The Christian may be able to accept a doctrinal statement, but find it necessary to interpret that statement according to his own personal Christian experience and how he verbalizes his experience.

If Christian theology is partly a set of questions, what can be asked about worship music? There are at least three:

1. What is the theological basis of worship music?

2. How does theology relate worship music to the total program of a church?

3. What theological criteria may be used for the evaluation of worship music?

THE THEOLOGICAL BASIS OF WORSHIP MUSIC

In most churches, the pastor is the resident theologian due to his theological education. Therefore, I am using "pastor" in place of "theologian" in the rest of this chapter. The pastor accepts music as a self-evident part of human life. Questions about the technical aspects of music are of no concern to him unless he is also a musician, or vitally interested in music, Theology does not give him or you criteria for the technical evaluation of worship music. However, when ultimate questions are asked about worship music and when music is incorporated into the life of a church, the pastor has a legitimate concern, for theological considerations are implied.

A basic theological concern is the definition of worship music. I define worship music as "music that is appropriate for the worship of a congregation." This means music is functional in the life of a church, a means to an end. Our rather broad definition indicates that almost any kind of music could be utilized within the worship of the church. It does not mean that almost any kind should be used. Appropriateness of the music used is dependent upon how worship is defined and actually practiced in particular churches.

Apart from this functional definition, no theological definition of worship music is possible. Music may have religious words or a religious title or even evoke a religious attitude and atmosphere. Yet, if this music is not appropriate for worship, it cannot be called "worship music" as I have defined it. Our thinking about the theological definition of worship music must be centered in how it functions in worship rather than in how it is composed.

THE SOURCE OF MUSIC

The pastor would assume that if music is known and understood, it is we who have perceived sound and called it music. If there is purpose in our music making, we have determined that purpose. If there is any value and significance in music, we have discovered this value and significance.

We are created in the image of God, and the thing that distinguishes us from lower animals is a quality of spirit. "God is spirit, and those who worship him must worship in spirit and truth" (John 4:24). We can worship the God who is spirit only because we are aware of spirit. We possess a human spirit, as believer's we possess the Holy Spirit, and we say things like "She's in good spirits today" or we refer to the spirit of an age or group of people

Within the limits of our life experiences, we are aware of this quality of spirit. As we exercise our spiritual responsibility to "fill the earth and subdue it; and have dominion" over all of nature (Gen. 1:28), we create morality, culture, and religion. Regardless of the form they take, these are all products of the human spirit.

If music is a product of our spirit, then all music is spiritual in this sense. As a human spiritual creation, music can and does speak to our spirits. As a human creation, music is finite and must be judged theologically as all other finite creations are judged. We create because God is creative. God has created out of Himself and is infinite, while we create out of what has been given to us in finite nature. Music is created within the depths of our spirit, but our human spirit is conditioned by a finite world; and the sound that we organize into music is also a part of the finite world.

WHAT IS EXPRESSED IN MUSIC?

Theologically, we are expressing ourselves, or at least some aspect of ourselves, through music. This is possible because we can control our environment, we can think, and we can put our thoughts into words. We can shape and change the objective world. This ability implies that we make both choices and value judgments about the world. We choose to shape, to change and modify, and to restructure our world.

We take sound, which is found in the external world, and shape that sound into music. Once music has been created, we can make choices and value judgments about that music. We can both change and modify or restructure the sounds used in music for our own purposes.

The quality of the human spirit expressed in music is of theological concern. As stated in the previous chapter, music is one way in which we attempt to rise above our finitude and to relate to the unconditioned elements of life. The pastor is concerned with the regeneration of the human spirit and how that new creation in Christ can find expression in culture.

Consequently, the pastor expects composers to be honest in their musical creations and to use their best efforts for musical self-expression. Musical honesty means to:

1. Compose music and write texts the best one knows how.

2. Perform and to accept a piece of music on the basis of its own characteristic style rather than to impose a style and/or characteristic upon it that is not an integral part of a piece of music.

3. Evaluate a piece of music by comparing it with other pieces of music in the same style and of the same type rather than comparing it with other styles and types of music. I cannot say a praise song is better than a hymn. I can say this praise song is better than that praise song or that hymn is better than this hymn.

4. Seek an understanding of what is expressed in a composition and to communicate that expression as accurately as possible in performance. This means any weakness the worship leader has in basic music skills and conducting will limit the ability to communicate music to others.

Musical honesty cannot always be determined by our personal reaction to a composition. If I do not like a certain kind of music, this does not necessarily mean the composer has not been honest, but perhaps means I do not possess either the musical sensitivity necessary to relate to the music properly or that I do not find personal self-expression in the music.

Musical honesty in worship music may be more apparent in vocal music since the verbal concepts expressed by a text can be analyzed and evaluated theologically. I have no theological criteria for the evaluation of musical honesty apart from a text and the response to music as it functions in worship. There are no sounds in music that I can identify as "church" sounds.

The absence of theological criteria for determining the technical honesty of music has produced a point of contention between many pastors and worship leaders. Often the worship leader has rejected a composition on musical grounds, while the pastor has accepted the same composition because of its text and suitability for worship. This had led to feelings of the pastor that the worship leader is insensitive to the theological meanings of texts and worship needs of people, and to feelings by the worship leader that the pastor is insensitive to musical values.

The musician may be critical of some worship music on the basis of both the music and the theological inadequacy of the text, while the pastor has accepted the same music because of its appeal to a congregation. Conceivably, a congregation could like and respond to a type of music unacceptable both to the pastor and the musician. It is also conceivable that a pastor could be completely insensitive to any kind of music. Hopefully, I would assume that you have sensitivity to spiritual values; else you would not be vocationally involved in worship music.

An attempt can be made to solve this dilemma in several ways. First, the cooperative efforts of both the pastor and the worship leader are required. They must agree upon what musical and spiritual values should be incorporated into a church's music program. This can be determined by asking two basic questions: What musical and spiritual skills, attitudes, and understandings do I wish to be a part of a person's mature Christian faith? And what specific musical and spiritual skills, attitudes, and understandings can be incorporated into the music program that will guide people toward this end?

Secondly, the church congregation needs to make a musical self-analysis to determine what is desired and needed musically in the church. If a church lacks the ability to make this self-analysis, the beginning point could be a program that would develop the ability. A well-selected worship and/or music committee can help you with this.

Thirdly, our desire for musical honesty should lead all people involved to the conclusion that music for worship should ideally be both a personal and a corporate self-expression. This same honesty should lead to the recognition that not all music is valid to all people as personal self-expression. This means that personal tastes might have to be submitted to the tastes and desires of the corporate body of the church.

Fourthly, if a congregation responds only to music that lacks spiritual depth both in text and music, this indicates that you and the pastor have a joint responsibility for enlarging the horizons of the people. You must each respect the experience and judgment of the other and have a spirit of genuine mutual trust.

THE NATURE OF THE MUSIC CREATION

The pastor understands music as a finite creation rather than something that can be elevated to the divine. Man's music making falls short of the glory of God regardless of how artistic or perfected that music making may be. No finite creation, no doctrine, and no church practice can ever attain equality with God or can express the reality of God in His fullness.

You cannot assume God will make Himself known in worship through any particular kind of music, or that He will be pleased with any particular kind of music. It is not music that must be worthy of God, but we ourselves. Too often we have concerned ourselves with the quality of music produced instead of the quality of those producing the music. We are worthy of God only through faith in Christ alone, which means we should respond with our praise and in giving to God our best efforts of service.

Your music is worthy of God only through this same faith. No finite creation is worthy of God in and of itself. Music does not validate itself in religious terms, but only in musical ones. Therefore, the greatest music, from the technical point of view, must be judged as being unworthy of God unless it is appropriated by you through your personal faith. Any theological significance of worship music must be supplied by you.

This does not mean you must make music as an act of faith, though this may well be true. What is meant is that music has worth before God only as it is an expression of your Christian faith and the faith of others using or apprehending music. This is what the writer of the Book of Hebrews was referring to when he said we should offer up a sacrifice of praise, "that is, the fruit of lips that acknowledge his [Christ's] name" (Heb. 13:15).

THEOLOGICAL PURPOSES OF WORSHIP MUSIC

Theologically, the purposes of worship music are the purposes of the church, namely, to meet human needs. People have many needs, but the church has the primary task of meeting human spiritual needs. Physical, social, and emotional needs must not be ignored, but are to be met within the context of the spiritual needs of people.

I cannot draw a one–to–one relationship between various human needs and church purposes without becoming artificial. There are at least four areas of spiritual need in which music can be of assistance in the life and work of a church: the need for conversion, for spiritual growth, for knowledge, and for fellowship.

THE NEED FOR CONVERSION

To the Christian, the need for conversion is the most basic need of humankind. All people strive to have their personalities organized around some focal point that will give meaning to life. We claim that this quest for meaning has not found its proper focal point until Christ becomes the center of life. This requires an experience of spiritual rebirth or conversion. This entails a radical change and reorientation of the total person with Christ as the center. The actual conversion experience has many forms, just as each personality is highly individualized. However, all conversion experiences involve repentance, faith, and regeneration by the Holy Spirit, in whatever form conversion is expressed outwardly.

Music can become a point of contact between the church and those in need of Christ. This might occur through the involvement of children in the choir program, and our evangelistic opportunities with and through children may not have been fully recognized. As a worship leader you have both the responsibility and the opportunity of sharing Christ with the children in their choirs. You might gain entrance to a non-Christian home that might not be open to others in the church because a child is active in music. Many children are attracted to church because of the music ministry and become prospects for other church organizations.

Music can become a point of contact between the church and those in need of Christ through their interest in music. A community oratorio choir, private music lessons, and music classes open to all are but a few of many opportunities for outreach through music.

Christians can share the gospel through music, and music can become the medium through which non-Christians respond to the invitation of Christ. Since the conversion experience is highly individual, no one type of music should be considered "evangelistic." We should utilize any type of music through which the Holy Spirit can speak to hearts in need.

THE NEED FOR SPIRITUAL GROWTH

Music is a big factor in PGBC!

The Bible teaches clearly that the new believer is a spiritual babe and needs to grow, for he or she has human potentialities that need to be developed if they are to be fruitful Christians. How does spiritual growth take place, and how does music function in this development?

First, we are to imitate Christ through the empowering of the Holy Spirit. All of us have a notion of what we would like to be, and all of our life activities are directed toward becoming this ideal or potential self. For Christians, the ideal self is exemplified in the life of Jesus and His teachings. At the same time we experience the struggle between the actual self (what we know ourselves to be) and the potential self (what we know we should be). This is the struggle described by Paul in Romans 7.

To imitate Christ requires us to be open to experience, to accept our actual selves at the moment, and try to do something with ourselves. Participating in music is a way of experiencing our actual selves at the moment, while at the same time voicing our aspirations for the ideal self. Music provides us with an opportunity to express our feelings and impulses symbolically, and it makes us aware of experiences in new and significant ways. Music should provide us with an opportunity to feel safe, to become our potential selves.

Second, spiritual growth comes as the Holy Spirit enables us to internalize our values. Being a Christian is not hiding behind a facade or keeping external rules. We are to be "led by the Spirit" (Rom. 8:14), and the entire thrust of the Book of Galatians is the freedom one has in Christ. Spiritual freedom also means spiritual responsibility (Gal. 5:13-14).

The creative person must feel free to make a self-evaluation and not have external judgments that say his creation is either "good" or "bad." At the same time, the person must assume responsibility for his creations. Others may react to the life of a person or things a person creates, but when the created product is labeled "good" or "bad," creative people are being told they cannot be themselves under God.

The New Testament teaches that the evaluation of one's life and how that life is expressed must be internalized by the Holy Spirit (see Hebrews 10:15-16; Luke 12:12; John 16:13; and Acts 2:17). This includes the application of the Scriptures as well, for they must become part of one's total self. The Scriptures are an invitation to share in the Christ life. The Scriptures present a reality system to be lived out, rather than information to be learned. The Spirit inspired the Scriptures, and the same Spirit interprets them to us and makes them part of us.

There are several implications for the church concerning the need for spiritual growth. These are implications for the person, for the church, and for the worship leader.

Implications for the person. Creativity is more than the production of "things." Creative acts may produce new attitudes of mind and heart or a new way at looking at oneself. We want Christian growth to take place in the hearts and lives of all Christians. As discussed previously, music is the product of one's spirit; if one's spirit grows, then he grows. If a person receives new insight into himself, about life, or about God through involvement in worship music, then spiritual growth could happen.

If participating in music is a way of experiencing our actual selves at the moment, while at the same time voicing our aspirations for the ideal self, the person must be free of external criticisms of his or her music makings. Whether making a "joyful noise" or singing with *bel canto*, each person should be encouraged to express feelings and impulses through music. Whether music participation is through performance or intelligent listening, everyone should feel safe to become potential selves through musical experience.

Implications for the church. The church as an organized and functioning body must be seen by its members as an actualization of themselves. A climate needs to be present in which the creativity of spiritual growth can take place in freedom and safety. Such a climate can be had if church members would accept each other as having unconditional worth, if external evaluation is absent, and if all try to understand one another empathically.

In such a situation you would be free to be creative and innovative in the music used, being free to experiment with many types of music. Only if you and the congregation are open to many kinds of music can music become an aid to spiritual growth.

It is always possible for a church to stifle the creativity that is part of spiritual growth. The history of Christianity is replete with examples of churches and denominations imposing restrictions not only upon music and the other arts, but upon scientific, philosophical, and other inquiry as well. A stifling of creativity will result in a stifling of spiritual growth and would indicate that a church or denomination lacks psychological and spiritual freedom and safety. Obviously, both you and the pastor must have personal psychological and spiritual freedom and safety and the willingness to guide a church toward that same freedom and safety.

Implications for the worship leader. First, and foremost, you must have a proper attitude toward those with whom you work. Each person must be accepted, as being of unconditional worth and understood empathically in so far is possible. People need to be challenged and encouraged to become their potential selves.

Second, you should try to help the congregation to internalize the criteria for the evaluation of music. You should not be the sole judge and arbiter of musical standards. This is particularly true in the use of terms such as "good," "bad," and "raise the standards" in connection with worship music. Not only are these terms ethical or moral in nature rather than musical; they are phrases that can hinder the climate of spiritual growth we are trying to foster. Musical honesty and our criteria for evaluating the adequacy of worship music materials would suggest that we use terms such as "better" and "broaden our repertoire" rather than negative ones.

Third, you must be open to all kinds of music that could conceivably be appropriate for a particular church. Consideration needs to be given to the consequences of rejecting any music or any composer because of a personal bias. This is especially true of contemporary music of all kinds. Can we afford to alienate a composer from Christ by saying music must be composed only in a particular way in order to be accepted by the church? There are no easy answers, but this and similar questions must be considered.

Fourth, the personal safety and freedom you enjoy must be matched by your sense of personal responsibility. Your individual freedom must never become a license to do what you want regardless of how your freedom affects the corporate life of the church. If you have attained some measure of spiritual growth and have experienced some degree of your potential self, you can accept responsibility and adapt to various situations in freedom.

THE NEED FOR KNOWLEDGE

one must retain knowledge!

For spiritual growth to follow conversion requires knowledge. This is knowledge that includes both understanding and how to apply what is known. The believer needs self-knowledge, knowledge of what is implied by the gospel, knowledge of life in terms of commitment to Christ, knowledge of the Scriptures, and knowledge of how to carry out the work of a church.

Beyond the self-knowledge which can come through music as an expression of our actual and potential selves, the Christian must have some skill in music making, since music functions within a church. Therefore, there is a need for the development of the basic skills of music making and attitudes about music and the role of music in the church. Music understandings would include the theological and biblical meanings of hymn and praise song texts.

Just as the members of a church will grow in their use of the Bible in relation to their ability to read, understand, and apply it to their daily lives, church members will grow in their use of music in relation to their ability to read, perform, understand, and respond to music. How well these needs are met will be in proportion to how aware you are to the needs of your people and your willingness to direct the music program of the church toward these ends.

THE NEED FOR FELLOWSHIP

This is an important factor!

The New Testament concept of *koinonia* is the Christian response to man's universal need for a loving, caring, and sharing fellowship. Salvation is a continuous experience and is developed within the context of other people. Ideally, a church is a teaching-learning-sharing group in which religious experience is given opportunity for development and maximum growth.

The essence of what a church is can be found in 1 John 1:7: "We have fellowship with one another." This word *koinonia* can be translated in several ways, but "sharing" is one of the best. Fellowship in a church is a sharing of the inner life. This is not the old life wrapped up in pious clothes, but something new and different. We cannot share what we do not have, and we cannot keep what we do have. We share our inner lives, our thoughts and feelings, our strengths and weaknesses, and our defeats and victories.

The basis of fellowship is the gospel of Christ, and we share a common experience in Christ, a common participation in God's grace and in the blessings of the Holy Spirit. Otherwise, there can be no fellowship. Fellowship, or sharing of oneself, involves communication. Communication requires some sort of vehicle through which communication takes place.

Communication involves symbols of various kinds, and music is one. Singing hymns and praise songs and hearing the texts of music sung can give the verbal concepts of Christian fellowship a quality that the words alone do not possess. This is why we sing hymns and songs rather than recite them together in worship. Music adds a quality of feeling both individually and corporately that the verbal concepts themselves do not possess.

THEOLOGICAL GUIDELINES FOR WORSHIP MUSIC

One of the questions raised earlier in this chapter was, "What theological criteria may be used for the evaluation of worship music?" I cannot give absolute criteria, but I can give several guidelines. Thinking about worship music theologically should give us an attitude about what worship music is, what its function is, and how it relates to the total life of a church. The following guidelines are suggestive of the attitudes you and I should have.

1. Three biblical concepts for our music making are: (a) I must have a proper attitude of mind and heart toward God; (b) God deserves and expects the very best of my efforts in all sincerity; (c) music must be related to the prophetic and educational tasks of the church.

2. Members of a church have the ability to make their own value judgments about worship music and must be encouraged to do so. At the same time, you and I have the obligation to guide members toward value judgments that are valid and meaningful to them both in musical and theological terms.

3. Church members need to know the relevance of music to themselves personally. This knowledge is acquired as they grow in the ability to make and to understand music, and as they are guided toward appropriate attitudes about music and their religious experience.

4. My theological frame of mind would protest against any attempt to make music either a completely rational or a completely emotional process. The rational and emotional aspects of music have both value and significance, but these do not give an ultimate meaning to music. Since music is in the realm of the human spirit and the divine Spirit, the real meaning of music includes both the rational and the emotional, but goes beyond them.

5. Thinking theologically should lead me to protest against any attempt to interpret worship music in any way that would identify the human response to music as the result of biological, social, or psychological factors alone. What constitutes "good music" can never be determined by a state, a church, a group, or a professional critic, but only by me. This judgment requires me to be competent through music training and experience to determine what is "good music."

6. I would emphasize that music is one of the deepest of human expressions. It must mean something to the person. One must be "grasped" by music and actively involved with it in a decisively personal manner.

7. I would emphasize that music represents one attempt on the part of persons to rise above our finitude and to project our potential selves onto an artistic symbol. Subsequently, theological perspective is needed to prevent us from substituting a musical elitism for a vital spiritual relationship with God through music that is available to all. This means the religious values of worship music must take precedence over artistic and musical values.

CHAPTER 5

YOU AND YOUR CULTURE

Culture has many definitions, most of which are really descriptions, such as: ethical society, human achievement, the world of values, the good for and of all persons, the temporal and material realizations of values, the conservation of values, and the pluralism of values. Perhaps we could define culture as the particular society in which we live with all of its behaviors, attitudes, knowledge, and material objects that are shared by and transmitted among members of that society.

As an art, music has relevance to different cultures. For a composer or performer, music may be one part of a very personal, private world. Yet, once music is presented publicly, it ceases to be part of the musician's exclusive domain. Society accepts or rejects music on the basis of its own values, and things may be "seen" and "heard" in the music that musicians neither intended nor thought of.

As stated earlier, a chasm has existed between the creative musician and the church far too often. The purpose of this chapter is to examine some possible societal reasons for this breach.

CONTEMPORARY SOCIAL PROBLEMS

There are many contemporary social problems, and the one reading this will know that those problems may have changed since the time of writing. Still, there seem to be recurring trends in contemporary life that affect the life of the church and the ministry of the church musician. Some of these are problems of:

1. Maintaining a common core of basic values in a multicultural world and trying to determine to what extent national values and goals can be preserved in an interdependent world.
2. Stem cell research and issues related to this research.

3. Conflicts between right to life and freedom of choice groups over abortion.

4. The changing status of women in the church.

5. Ecology and the conservation of natural resources.

6. The influence of popular culture on the music choices, values and moral behavior of young people.

7. The influence of popular culture on worship practices in the church.

These problems of contemporary culture have implications for the worship leader. When you join a church staff you bring a culture with you. You enter a church culture that is an amalgam of the various cultures brought to the church by its membership. Somehow we need to understand our personal cultural biases and the cultural biases of the people with whom we work. As servant leaders in the church we must learn to lay aside our personal cultural biases and work within the culture of the church.

Perhaps the social issue that will affect the work of the worship leader most is in the area of popular music culture. This culture includes a wide array of music types and musical icons. Popular culture is commercially driven. Commercial interests can influence the criteria for the selection of worship music: the record companies, publishing companies and various Christian performing groups and soloists. It is a problem for some of the Christian performers, too, for if enough records are not sold, they could very well be dropped from a recording company's roster.

In a popular culture art music is less important to the average person than popular music as evidenced by a comparison of record sales and admission tickets to concerts. Art music does not produce a product of commercial value except to a small group of people.

This affects church music, since the only formal training in music to large numbers of people in a community is that given by a church. The future state of music in the churches is the sole responsibility of the worship leader. Consequently, the worship leader must have the ability to arrange music, to conduct, to lead and to teach others. These skills are based upon a solid foundation in music theory, of keyboard skills and in personal performance.

Current cultural changes have resulted in a large variety of responses from those in the churches. Some people have defended themselves against the forces of change by retiring to the traditional past in doctrine and church life and defending the tradition zealously. In music, they demand the familiar and comfortable whether the music and its texts are particularly relevant to the present or not.

Others have accepted the newer cultural situation and have tried to adapt themselves to it by reinterpreting their beliefs in more contemporary terms. However, contemporary musical expression is limited mainly to a more contemporary popular style, such as the short, easily sung chorus based directly upon a biblical text.

There are those few who have accommodated themselves to contemporary culture and have proclaimed the new as a direct involvement of God within human history. These people would accept the more artistic forms of contemporary music as valid expressions of religious faith.

Several questions are implied in these responses to culture that are of concern to the worship leader:

1. What is the relationship between the cultural responses of church members and the style and/or manner of music and worship they prefer?
2. How is one's attitude toward cultural change reflected in the music and worship he or she desires?
3. Does the mass media have a positive or negative effect on the type of church music we can use?
4. Can a church music program be successful without a primary reference to the quality of each person's musical and religious experiences?
5. Does the church have any responsibility to preserve, advance, and continue music as an "art," or should the church bow to popular tastes?
6. Does the music program of the church exist primarily for aesthetic, musical, social, evangelistic, or worship purposes? On what basis can this be determined?

Definitive answers are impossible to give. However, tentative answers may be discovered by a study of the problems of Christian responses to culture, music as a cultural creation, and the role of the composer in a society.

CHRISTIAN RESPONSES TO CULTURE

Christians have always found it difficult to relate properly to the culture in which they live. They discover they "are in the world, but not of the world." The problem is more intense for worship leaders since music is produced, received, and affected by culture at the same time one is trying to relate this art to the church. As an organization, the church is a part of culture and is subject to the same theological and biblical judgment as any other part of culture. The church and its music is no more immune to the judgment of God than any other aspect of a culture.

The effectiveness of the music ministry in a church depends in large measure upon the cultural responses and values of those who make up the membership of a church. What is the proper relationship between the church and culture? Between the believer and culture? or, more importantly, Between Christ and culture?

Both the individual believer and the church are grounded upon the person of Christ. Consequently, we must look at the problem of Christ and culture and define both Christ and culture before we can seek solutions. Different schools of contemporary theology define Christ in various ways. Most scholars would agree that Jesus was a prominent figure in history and would probably agree upon the salient facts of His life: His exhibition of unconditional love, His eternal hope, His complete obedience to God, His faith, and His humility. To the evangelical Christian, the only term adequate to describe Jesus is: the Son of God. Belief in Jesus is a particular belief in and about God and about the church as the body of Christ.

There have been some historical responses of Christians to their culture. In his book *Christ and Culture* Richard Niebuhr gave three: Christ against culture; Christ of culture; and Christ above culture.

CHRIST AGAINST CULTURE

The first response to the problem of Christ and culture is a rejection of culture. The basic idea of this position is: Christ has founded a new order and is its Lawgiver and King. Culture is sinful in itself and must be avoided in order to protect the identity of the new community of faith.

Both Christ's teachings and other biblical teachings seem to indicate the necessity of the believer to forsake culture and cling only to Christ in faith. Fundamentalists and extreme conservatives hold to this view. Since culture is sinful one should not play cards, go to movies, etc. No music should be used in church which can be closely identified with the secular world. The "old songs" are preferred over anything new in music since the "old" is tried and proven to be trustworthy.

While those holding this position are sincere and do much in the way of evangelism and missions support, it is an inadequate solution to the problem of Christ and culture. The person of Christ can be lost in the legalism of the new community of faith: His laws are more important than His nature and love, and the idea of personal and corporate sin is blurred by the overpowering evil of the surrounding world. By avoiding the world, many feel they have avoided sin.

Christians cannot entirely reject culture, for they are part of it and express themselves with ideas derived from culture. It is impossible to reestablish a first-century culture and to mold our beliefs and practices to it. Even the "old songs" take on the rhythms and harmonies of the present age. The result is a Christian subculture which is isolated from the prevailing culture. We need to ask, Is the kingdom of God limited only to those who have been "separated"? Is the sovereignty of God over the universe determined solely on the basis of whether or not mankind receives his revelation in faith? Can one's musical expression of faith be limited only to that of previous generations?

THE CHRIST OF CULTURE

The second response is that of identifying Christ with a specific culture as the Messiah of that culture. Christians with this concept sense no conflict between church and world or faith and works. Jesus is interpreted as the Creator and Sustainer of culture. Culture includes only those things considered to be good.

Christ focuses upon the forgiveness of sins, culture upon the ethical striving toward perfection. Loyalty to Christ leads to active participation in cultural activity. Humans are giving battle to an impersonal nature, mostly outside themselves. Jesus is the great emancipator and is identified with the finest ideals, noblest institutions, and best philosophies.

This has been a view in church music: Only music of the highest artistic value is worthy of the worship of God. The aesthetic response to artistic music is the same as religious awareness and commitment to God. God inspires "beautiful" music, and we find Him revealed as we become involved with this music.

Apart from the theological inadequacy of this view, we must object to it on musical grounds as well. Who and what determine the nature of music? As stated earlier, the worth of music before God lies in the faith of the one producing and using the music. As a human creation, music has no worth before God in and of itself.

If religious experience and aesthetic experience are the same, how is one converted? True, we can have a religious experience through music, but only because we have had an initial conversion experience. It is only the conversion experience that enables us to have religious experiences through music that are solely and uniquely Christian experiences.

If religious and aesthetic experiences are the same, what is the nature of the God we worship and experience? Unless we experience the God who is revealed through the Scriptures, through Christ, and through the Holy Spirit, our God becomes music.

Music has the ability to move people both emotionally and intellectually. Herein lies both the strength and weakness of church music. The music produced in church could become an end in itself rather than a means to an end if emotional and intellectual stimulation is all that is produced or required. Such a situation could result in the loss of real spiritual power that could come through music.

When music moves people we cannot know whether this results from the work of the Holy Spirit or from sentimentality or nostalgia. This is why musical honesty in our music making is so essential. We can only pray that God will choose to use our music as a medium for empowering His own.

CHRIST ABOVE CULTURE

The third response to the problem of Christ and culture is to place Christ above culture. This response has had three main representative groups: those who synthesize Christ and culture, which is the traditional Roman Catholic position; those who place Christ and culture in paradoxical tension, which is the traditional Lutheran and neo-orthodox viewpoint; and those who see in Christ a redeemer of culture, which is not represented by any one denomination or group of theologians. Many concerned theologians of evangelical persuasion hold to this view within all major Protestant denominations.

The synthesis of Christ and culture. Those who hold this view believe the problem is not one of Christ and culture, but a problem of man and God. Christ cannot be opposed to His creation; therefore, culture is not the place of evil in itself since it is founded upon the world of divine creation. Human works cannot be separated from the grace of God, since it is through works that persons make themselves worthy of receiving that divine grace.

Saint Clement defined a Christian as one who first became a good man in accordance with cultural standards: Christ uses the instruments of culture to give persons what they cannot attain alone. Saint Thomas rejected the secular world, but became the guardian of a culture that produced the rich, secular Roman Catholic Church against which the Reformers rebelled.

The church stands above culture in an untouched cultural world of its own. The church is the guardian of God's grace and dispenses it through the sacraments.

Attempts to retain plainsong in the Catholic Church and various papal encyclicals dealing with church music up to Vatican II have created a musical culture that is supposedly distinct from secular musical culture. Changes since Vatican II leave the question open for the moment since Catholics are struggling to relate newer cultural expressions of music to their view of sacramental grace.

Christ and culture in paradox. This view states there is a conflict between God and humanity. On one side is all of our culture, including the church; on the other side is God. The starting point is the redemptive act of Christ in history. Humanity is sinful before God, and not even a church can be worthy of the Lord's attention or devotion. Therefore, no matter how sincerely humans try to please God, they are corrupt.

In contrast to the Catholic view, this Lutheran viewpoint sees reason as being corrupt and calls attention to the will within a person that would make him become his own God. Not even the monastery could remove this will, and to synthesize Christ and culture by the use of reason (and the sacraments) is forming a new depraved culture, hiding behind Christianity.

Luther taught there were two related kingdoms: the kingdom of God and the kingdom of Caesar. He said further that the Christian must affirm both. Culture is merely the sphere in which Christ operates. The problem is, "How must a Christian operate within culture?"

In music Luther would say that we must affirm the very best music culture can produce, and at the same time affirm the very best music that is a witness to the gospel. This paradoxical tension is almost as great as that produced by those who place Christ against culture. How can the church musician affirm the best music culture produces and at the same time select music that is a valid witness to the gospel? In what ways can the music of culture be a witness to the gospel?

Christ the redeemer of culture. Those who follow this line of thought hold much in common with the others of the Christ above culture school. Perhaps a better term would be "conversionist," since the emphasis is upon the Redeemer character of Christ.

The conversionist holds three basic theological assumptions:

a   We live in a created world under the sovereign rule of the Creator; God is King whether we recognize Him or not;

b.   Original sin and human nature are not evil in themselves, but perverted goods;

    c.   History is not a record of the course of human events, but is a record of the interaction between God and persons. The Bible is the inspired source of that record.

In John's Gospel we find a contrast to Jesus' response to God the Father, and the world's response, not to God, but to the devil. The world is not evil in itself, but is paying allegiance to the wrong master (John 8). Redemption is putting this allegiance right.

If we recognize that the very best of our efforts in music are in reality perverted goods, then we can recognize that any and all types of music could be used in world redemption. If we look at church music history not as a record of the course of musical events, but as a record of the interaction of God and man through music, we can be made aware of many different types of church music and willing to use different types of church music in our worship.

Many people would claim that Niebuhr's work is dated and no longer relevant. Perhaps in some instances, but you will discover many people in your church who would represent one or more of these reactions to culture. The current reaction to culture has been termed "postmodernism."

POSTMODERNISM

Postmodernism is a broad term that is applied to several areas of learning, particularly in the humanities. It is a reaction to the assumed certainty of scientific, or objective, efforts to explain reality. In religion it is a reaction to the assumed certainty of theology as explaining the nature of God and the way of salvation. Postmodernists are skeptical of any explanation that claims to be valid for all cultures, groups, traditions and races. Postmodernism claims reality only comes into being through our personal interpretations of what the world means to us.

Postmodernism is "post" because it denies the existence of any ultimate realities or principles. There is no scientific, philosophical or religious truth that will explain everything for everybody. It is interesting that by placing all ultimate truths and realities under scrutiny even the principles of postmodernism are open to question.

Some Christian leaders have developed what is called "emergent worship" as a means of reaching out to those of the postmodern generation. Faith is described in terms of a journey. Faith is a struggle to trust God rather than acceptance of a set of beliefs. Popular culture is the field into which God sends His laborers to reap the harvest. Popular culture is not something to be conquered or protected. Music leaders are not focal points of the congregation's attention and sermons are not the focal point of the worship experience.

Conclusion. Regardless of the personal position we take in relation to the problem of Christians responding to culture, it seems we could have a credo summed up in three statements. First, we need an absolute faith in God through Christ in the face of our current social uncertainties. Second, we need to choose and to use the best music for use in the church with our best understanding in view of the local church's social situation. Third, we make free choices in our music by trusting God at the same time. Christian freedom is depending upon God.

MUSIC AS A CULTURAL CREATION

Church music is a product both of culture and religion. We have defined culture as a particular society in which we live with all of its behaviors, attitudes, knowledge, and material objects that are shared by and transmitted among members of that society. The institutional aspects of religion can be contained within that definition.

Religion of any kind is thought to be our relationship to divine beings, whose existence theologians assert. Since divine beings do not exist in culture, how can we have a relationship with something culturally nonobjective? The only things existent objectively in culture are ideas about divine beings; and, as such, these ideas are a part of culture.

Christian faith cannot be defined in this way. Let us take, instead, the presupposition that religion is an aspect of the human spirit. This means that if we look at the human spirit from one particular viewpoint it appears to us as religious. This particular view is the point from which we can look into the depth of our spiritual life. Religion is not a "special" function of the human spirit, but is the dimension of depth that is present in all of the functions of the human spirit, including art, politics, morality, etc.

As stated earlier, when we confront our universe, we are aware of something unconditioned, something over which we have little or no control. As Christians, we hold the conviction that only God is unconditioned.

The significance of this for the church musician is in our awareness of the unconditioned elements in the musical creations of culture. Anyone who has put their hand to composing music is painfully aware that there are many aspects of musical materials that do not yield completely to our human control. This is true in performance as well. Consequently, as worship leaders, let us start with a broad definition of religion: that all of life and the creations and expressions of life are basically religious because of our inability to control the unconditioned. Such a definition has three consequences.

First, it enables the Christian musician to confront the secular musician with the fact that the secular musician is religious, though he may reject organized religion or the Christian faith. The problem with his religion is what he considers to be ultimate. We make the claim that only the God who revealed himself within and under the conditions of human existence in Jesus Christ is worthy of ultimate and unconditioned concern.

Second, this broad definition enables us to eliminate sacred and secular music into separate realms of culture. This is not saying the gap between the Christian and the secular in culture has been closed. Secularism is a religion in whatever form it takes and has ideas and objects that are sacred. The ultimate choice is between the sacred of Christianity and the sacred of secularism and the music produced by both.

Third, it enables us to see that religion is what gives meaning to a culture. Secular culture is as impossible as atheism, since both presuppose something unconditioned in life. Whenever we recognize the unconditioned element either in ourselves, in the world, or in music, we are being religious, but not necessarily Christian.

On the basis of this understanding of religion, Christian musicians can look anew at all types and forms of music. The products of culture should not be rejected, accommodated to, or ignored, but should be redeemed. As an unknown Christian leader is quoted as saying, "Why should the devil have all the best tunes!" The proper understanding of humanity and our relationship to our spiritual creations can give the Christian musician insight into how the redemption of humans can be accomplished.

The difficulty we have in accepting newer forms of music is because they are autonomous. The autonomous person is captain of his own soul; he lives by the rational structure of his own mind and makes his own laws. Autonomy seeks the freedom and dignity of the person. Sadly, though, the autonomous state is impotent to satisfy our inner needs and leaves us cut off from our roots – frustrated and in despair.

Aleatory or "chance music" is a prime example of autonomous music. Aleatory composers are concerned with eliminating the barriers that exist between the performer and listener and between the composer, performer, and listener. Within broad general guidelines the individual performer and the individual listener are encouraged to explore their own subjectivity. At the same time, the composer is exploring his own subjectivity by establishing the broad musical guidelines for others to follow. The concern is for personal expression, and not for the proclamation of any particular "message."

Much contemporary Christian music is autonomous. When derived from secular rock music contemporary Christian music and musicians have elements of rebellion, individuality and a "stick it in your eye" attitude of secular rock music.

The biblical ideal is for the superior law given by God to be at the same time the innermost law of persons. This law of God is not imposed from without, but is discovered within persons through reconciliation with God through faith in Christ. The result would be a culture that was transparent to the presence of God. This is the kingdom of God actualized in people. Such a culture would be ruled by agape love through the Holy Spirit, and the products of that culture would let God be seen through them.

This is why we defined church music as that which is appropriate for the services of a church. There is no "sacred" or "secular" music. There is only music; and some of that music can be used of the Spirit to make God known. The degree to which the Spirit can work is dependent upon our ability to select music that adequately expresses our relationship to God.

THE COMPOSER IN SOCIETY

The composer, whether of art music, rock or contemporary Christian music, grasps and shapes reality in a composition that is the direct artistic expression of his or her ultimate concern. The music is shaped in such a way that the public can find an expression of its ultimate concern as well. This raises the old problem: Which is the real piece of music, that which the composer has put on the score or that which is heard when the music is performed?

Composing music is indescribable; it is the unknown that we must recognize as unknowable until it happens. It is the improbable until it becomes probable. A composer desires to communicate and to share his creation, even if he has to organize or imagine such a group.

However, the composer does not create in order to communicate to others. He has been compelled by inner necessity to create a new aspect of himself in relation to his environment. Once having created, he desires to share this new aspect of himself with others.

Once a composition has been released to the public, meanings will be given the work that the composer did not intend. He is probably unaware of all that he has released in the work, either in terms of its deficiencies or of its positive values. The composition has an objective existence of its own and an intentional character of its own. This is true of all types of music.

Our concern should be in the objective, intentional character of the music itself. Too often, people will say about a new piece of music, "But I don't see or hear anything in the music." By this they mean they are unable to discern the technical problems worked out or a story that is told. Instead, they should be concerned with what the music says to and for them, and how.

CHAPTER SUMMARY

Again, we have raised more problems in this chapter than given answers. Yet, there are some conclusions to be made regarding music as an objective cultural creation.

We need to define religion broadly: that all of life and the creations and expressions of life are basically religious.

- As Christian musicians we should not be as concerned with music that is sacred or secular, but with music which is transparent to the presence of God. This is music that can express our relationship to God and through which God can reveal Himself.

- Music that is transparent to God is not something that can be deliberately created, but must be discovered. When a person participates in and with music, and finds in that music an artistic expression of his inner life as a believer, he has discovered music that is transparent.

- There is no sacred and secular music as such, except by usage. Our best efforts in music are really perverted goods, rather than evils in themselves. Consequently, any and all types of music could be used in world redemption.

- If a composer expresses an aspect of himself in relation to his environment, the public can also find a musical expression in its relationship to environment. If the word God is substituted for the word environment, we can see the implications of this for Christian music. This also indicates that the public must both accept the integrity of the composer and know how this relationship is expressed musically.

- The ability of the public to relate itself properly to a piece of music is relative to the ability of persons to understand and to articulate the expressive and structural forms of music. The composer has expressed himself through the elements of music. He can be understood only to the degree that the listener is able to comprehend these same elements for himself.

- Christians have a problem of how to relate to their culture, and five possible responses to culture were presented.

- Because religion has been defined in the narrow sense of Christian faith, there has been no basis for dialogue with the non-Christian musician. This has resulted in a false division of music into sacred and secular, the sacred being music which can be easily associated with the ideas of the Christian faith. A broader definition of religion would eliminate this division and give us a basis for dialogue.

- We have been too intent upon discovering the technical aspects of music composition and performance without concern for that part of himself the composer is expressing, and what part of ourselves the music is expressing.

- We can only make contact with the composer and his music when we discover what of himself he is expressing in his music and why.

CHAPTER 6

YOU ARE A MUSIC TEACHER

A primary task of the worship leader is to develop the music skills, knowledge, and understandings of church members. If this does not happen, the function of music in a church will be inadequate. You may have received little or no training in teaching techniques and have had little opportunity to study learning theories or to develop a basis for enlarging upon their teaching techniques. However, you cannot escape this responsibility of teaching if you are a worship leader. Even if you have limited musical ability, you are still a music teacher when you stand before a congregation or choir or praise band and lead them in music.

People learn music in two ways. First, we have to have some basic skills to perceive sound as music. Second, everyone learns by thinking reflectively and reasonably about music. We do not learn music and then think about it. This is not step one and step two. Skill development and thinking about music is required at each level of music learning, whether with pre-school children or university students.

PERCEIVING MUSIC AS SOUND

Perception is the gaining of knowledge directly through the senses. To perceive music is to see, hear, and feel melody, harmony, rhythm, form, and expression in music. How we perceive is dependent upon many things and is strictly personal.

Psychologists have discovered that we engage in various activities in order to come to an understanding of what we perceive. In learning music, the person must have many opportunities to encounter music through various learning activities and through many types of music literature. Since music is sound, it is perceived primarily through hearing. However, what we see and feel in our encounter with many types of music also influences what and how we hear.

Intelligence is the result of our perceiving things and then modifying them in different ways. This is a process of "thinking about" things in which we review, recall, and elaborate upon what we have perceived, and memorize signs and terms that will assist us in future learning. Finally, we can use the new ideas we have learned in perceiving new things.

The perception of music occurs at four different levels, each building upon the one that came before it. These four levels of perception are logical in sequence and not chronological. All four levels may be present at the same time to some degree in music perception.

The first level of music perception is the *responsive level*. This is the level on which we respond to music by patting a foot, humming, clapping, etc. This is the level at which we are primarily concerned with seeing, hearing, and feeling music without any attempt to explain it.

The *associative level* of music perception is the level on which one associates his musical responses with nonmusical events and ideas. We associate what we see, hear, and feel in the music with personal images and stories. We know, for example, when the hero of a movie is going to be hit on the head in a dark alley because of the background music. We have learned to associate certain kinds of music with danger.

The *analytical level* of music perception is the level on which we are able to analyze and to compare different kinds of music. This is thinking about the music and making value judgments about the music. The person decides for himself why the music moves or sounds in a particular way and whether or not the music has any meaning and/or significance for him.

The average person seems to have a natural ability to respond to music in an elementary way. But in order to develop complete music understanding, a person must be able to discriminate between melody, harmony, and rhythm in one piece of music and compare these elements to other pieces of music.

To tell one kind of music from another requires this ability to discriminate. Most people have little difficulty in catching simple tunes and distinguishing between different tunes, but more complex tunes are more difficult to perceive only by listening. More complex music requires some ability to understand the printed score and to compare different scores.

The highest level of music perception is the *autonomous*. This is the level on which we are able to contemplate the formal elements of music for their own sake apart from any practical values or benefits the music might have. This is the level of perception that we could call musicality or musical intelligence and which involves independent music making by the person, such as performing and creating music.

GUIDING THE PERCEPTION OF MUSIC

Learning is growth, and all growth can be developed and guided. Teaching is a process of guiding development so growth takes place. In order to guide growth we must have some desired behaviors toward which we aim. Growth implies there are various states of development and that the person can move from one state to another.

Behavior includes actions, understandings, concepts, appreciations, and skills. If learning takes place, then behavior changes. We do not know what happens when a person learns, for there are no organic changes that can be detected or described as one learns. Therefore, we infer learning has taken place because of a change in behavior. We can define behavior either as an observable act or acts, or an observable product of an act or acts. When a person is able to play the fifteen major scales on the piano that he has previously been unable to play, the observable act is his performance. When a composer writes a new piece of music the new composition is the observable product of behavior.

As a change in observable behavior, learning must be either the acquisition of new behavior or the extension of previous behavior. As we stated previously, the process of learning in itself is not behavior because we cannot see what is going on inside the person. Learning is what we infer from outward behavior.

Obviously, not any observable behavior is related to learning. We may see a man rake leaves in his yard, then stop and put his rake in the garage and go indoors. There has been an observable change of behavior, but not related to learning since there has been neither an extension of previous behavior or the acquiring of new behavior.

LEARNING MUSIC SKILLS

In the process of learning music skills we are teaching people to perform muscle skills. It is a matter of muscular development to the point that one can perform the skill.

Teaching music skills involves identifying the separate acts that make up the total skill, then listing them in the sequence in which the separate acts are performed to make up the total act. An example would be learning to change a tire on a car. First, you make sure the hand brake is set. Then what do you do? After that, what? Once this sequence has been determined, we would teach a person by going through the steps in sequence. People learn skills in the following sequence:

1. They are given a model of the total motor skill expected.

2. They are given a model of each separate act involved in the total skill that is required.

3. They identify the separate acts to be performed in their sequence.

4. Through guided practice by the teacher, they explore each separate act and the total skill.

5. They are given corrective feedback from the teacher during practice.

6. They must have adequate repetitive practice with enough duration to develop habitual performance and with enough frequency that the skill is not lost.

Skill level depends upon how well muscular coordination and the bodily sensations associated with proper performance have been developed. This whole idea will be made more understandable if you will think through how you have been taught to play an instrument or to sing. We must keep in mind, too, that the development of skills in music is never isolated from thinking about music. Ideally, skills and thinking like a musician will be in balance.

THINKING CRITICALLY ABOUT MUSIC

Music has a logic that enables us to think about it reflectively. The trained musician thinks in terms of the logic of music, either consciously or unconsciously. He or she knows and uses a technical vocabulary to explain and describe music. The trained musician thinks reflectively about the context in which music is created and how that context impinges upon both the creation and recreation of music. Musicians ask a set of questions that determine how music will be created and recreated.

In thinking reflectively and reasonably about the elements of musical thought, I am using the elements of reasoning developed by Richard Paul. In fact, I will borrow the way he and Linda Elder have stated it in their book *Critical Thinking: Tools for Taking Charge of Your learning and Your Life*"[p. 53]:

Whenever you are reasoning,
you are trying to accomplish some purpose,
within a point of view,

using concepts or ideas.
You are focused on some issue or question or problem,
using information
to come to conclusions,
based on assumptions,
all of which has implications

PURPOSE

When we think, we do so with a purpose. What is the purpose of musical thought? It is to think about sound: how to make sound, how to organize and control sound and how to reproduce the sounds we are trying to organize and control. Music was born when people began thinking about the sounds they heard. Centuries of musical thought have resulted in a highly specialized system of symbols and language cues that have enabled us to organize and control sound in ways that have produced many kinds of music.

The purpose of musical thought can be extended to thought about music in specific contexts. We can think about what is appropriate music for worship. We can think about the kind of music to use for entertainment, weddings, funerals and a host of other contexts. When people are actively engaged in "doing" music they experience what it means to act and think like a musician.

POINT OF VIEW

We reason from a particular point of view that reflects our orientation to the world. The training needed if one is to become a professional performer, teacher or composer influences a musician's point of view.

What is a musician's point of view? In general, the professional musician is oriented toward the highest level of creating, performing and listening to music. He or she has to look at the world from many points in time and different cultures. This requires highly developed skills and well-trained practitioners and musicians are involved in a life-long pursuit of personal excellence. The way we teach people and the expectations we have for them are shaped by the professional point of view of excellence in creating, performing and listening to music.

Another point of view is prevalent in many churches, and that is the idea that worship leaders do not need to be highly trained musicians. This is a point of view that the church can get by on second or third best. Some would say, "That's alright for schools to require high standards, but the church does not need that."

Why should we not expect the highest level of creating and performing music in the church? Does not God deserve the best? Does not God require more of us?

Concepts

A concept is a complete and meaningful idea that is in the mind of a person, a mental image of what one has perceived through the senses. Concepts are subjective to each person and are based upon one's own personal situation and experiences. Concepts are expressed in verbal statements that describe one's mental conceptualization. However, a discrepancy may exist between what one is able to verbalize and what his actual conceptualization may be. A five-year-old may have valid concepts but lack the vocabulary to verbalize his conceptualization.

Statements of concepts to be learned need to be defined as clearly as possible and stated in simple, concise sentences. Until the learner has experienced those aspects of music from which concepts have been derived, conceptualization cannot take place. When a person is unable to verbalize his conceptualizations, we could refer to this as a preconceptual or a general awareness state in learning. We do not teach concepts; we teach from concepts; and we try to get the learner to develop his own statements that make sense to him.

Learning theorists have organized human learning into three domains: the cognitive (what a person knows); the psychomotor (what a person does): and the affective (what and how a person feels). The three domains are not exclusive of each other, but are interrelated. Concepts lie in the cognitive domain, but conceptualization is required for the acquisition of skills and values as well as of concepts. Conceptualization of music is a process of

1. Thinking that helps the person to identify uniqueness in a music event, such as a climax or the repetition of material. It is made easier when the learning activities cause the person to think about the music.

2. Recognizing ways in which various musical elements are the same, similar, and different, such as phrasing and rhythm patterns.

3. Identifying the functional relationships between musical events, such as the relationship between chords and melodies or the relationship between cadences and form.

A specialized vocabulary is used to interpret, classify and sort information about music. The basic concepts of music are rhythm, pitch, shape and expression. These terms are descriptors of how sounds and silences are organized and controlled. *Rhythm* is the element that gives us a sense that the music is "moving." The concept of rhythm includes the other concepts of beat, duration, accent, meter and tempo.

Pitch in music refers to the lows and highs of music sounds and includes melody, scales and harmony. Other concepts that help us label pitch are key, tonality and pitch names. Pitch also includes the idea of timbre, the individual sound of a specific instrument or voice.

Shape is how music appears to us as sound, and is usually referred to as form. There are many of these forms and have names such as minuet-and-trio, rondo and symphony. These words all describe a different way of organizing sounds and silences in an understandable shape.

Expression is how music expresses something to us and something for us. We use adjectives to describe these expressions, such as fast–slow, high–low, and happy–sad. There is nothing to "see" or to "read" in music as in other art forms. Music depends solely upon hearing, so a listener must learn what to listen for. Music performers learn how to convey the expression intended by the composer.

Musical expression also involves *style,* the way composers at a specific time write music in a particular way. Style in music is like style in clothing or hair or cars or anything else. From your own experience you can tell the difference between opera and country-western music. That difference is style.

QUESTIONS IN MUSIC

Thinking is directed toward a question to be answered or a problem to be solved. If our purpose is to think about sound, what questions and problems are there?

Early humans began asking questions about the sounds they heard. What was that sound? What kinds of sound did I hear? How was it made? Who or what made the sound? How can I make that sound? What would happen if I combined this sound with that sound? How are the sounds organized? How can I organize sound? These questions raised by the earliest humans are still valid, but they have been greatly expanded until there are many special categories of music study that are driven by their own set of questions.

The breadth of the questions asked in musical thinking can be illustrated by the following:

- Who makes music?
- Why is music made?
- Where is music made?
- How is music made?
- When is music made?
- What kinds of music are made?

The depth of the questions raised in musical thinking can be illustrated by the following examples:

- What was/is the composer doing with sound?
- What part of him/herself is the composer expressing in the music?
- Why is one piece of music better than another?
- Why is one performance of music better than another?
- How does music affect human emotion and behavior?
- How important is music in society?
- Who should pay for music to be created and performed?
- Does music have anything to do with morality?
- Should music be censored?
- What is the difference between music as a fine art and music as a popular art?

Some of the questions have become blurred and made more difficult to answer because the delineation between music as a fine art and music as a popular art has become blurred. For example, if we ask the question: "Why is this piece of music better than that piece of music?" we must ensure that we are comparing the same genre of music. To compare Beethoven with the Beatles would not produce an objective, rational answer. Only when we raise the question why one Beethoven piece is better than that Beethoven piece could a rational answer be given. While disagreement might still arise about which is the better piece Beethoven composed, the question does lead to a reasoned judgment.

INFORMATION

What information is needed to answer these questions? The system of notation and verbal cues used by composers to create music is the most fundamental information needed. In addition one must understand the ways musical sound has been and is organized and controlled by specific composers.

The musician needs to know the various ways musical sound has been and is organized and controlled within a particular historical and cultural context. He or she must be familiar with representative music literature that is available for analysis and performance both from specific composers and from various historical and cultural contexts. Musicians must learn about the many ways music is made by individuals, groups, instruments and electronic tone generators.

CONCLUSIONS

All thinking has implication, conclusions and/or consequences and music is no exception. What are some conclusions to be drawn from thinking reflectively about music? Some conclusions are reached about the sounds of music:

- The basic concepts of pitch, rhythm, shape and expression have organized and controlled sound throughout history within the context of a given culture.

- Some pitches have an acoustical tendency to move in a particular direction.

- Some chords have an acoustical tendency to move to other specific chords.

- People have continually sought ways of organizing and controlling sound.

- The way sounds and silences are organized and controlled is relative to the historical and cultural context that produces the music.

Other musical conclusions relate to the affects of musical sound:

- Music can be both meaningful and significant to the person without verbal or visual stimuli.

- Music gives the impression of movement though tension-release, harmonic progression, tonal/melodic patterns and periodic rhythm patterns.

- Music can be meaningful and significant in itself and/or by association with non-musical events and stories.

- By reflectively thinking about music, everyone has the capacity to make personal value judgments about music.

- People make different kinds of music in different ways and in different places.

ASSUMPTIONS

Our reasoning is based upon those things we take for granted, the things we assume to be true and need no proof. What are some musical assumptions that musicians base their conclusions on? Look at these examples:

- Music is organized and controlled sounds and silences moving in time.

- Music is a universal art, requiring no language but its own for people to respond to in meaningful and significant ways.

- Music is the way people in various places and various times have organized sound in ways that express their deepest feelings.

- People can make a physical response to music.

- Most people can find meaning and significance both in music they hear and music they make.

- Most people can grow in their ability to understand music and respond to it.

- Music is a common experience of all peoples everywhere.

- The specialized vocabulary of music enables a person to speak and write about the music they experience.

IMPLICATIONS

The implications for thinking about music are improved performance and improved understanding of music. Ways of developing music in the church are implied. Rehearsal time can be spent on interpretation rather than dealing with problems of music reading. Members of performing groups will be able to convey the expressive elements of the music they perform. The entire church music program will be able to enhance the worship of the church through better performance

WAYS OF DEVELOPING MUSIC IN THE CHURCH

Not everyone is or will become a professional musician. They will be those people who support the opera, symphony orchestras and music education in the schools. They will be the people who sing in your choir or worship team and play in your praise band. They will be the people who sit in your congregation. Learning to think critically about music enables these people to appreciate music and to make personal value judgments about the music they hear.

If anyone in the church is to learn by thinking, worship leaders need to ask questions that require people to think more broadly and deeply about the music information they receive, the music they hear and their emotional interactions with music. As teachers we can learn to ask three kinds of questions.

First, there are questions that call for statements of fact, or one-system questions. In one-system questions there is an established procedure for finding the answer. Facts and definitions or both are used to give a definite answer. In music these are questions that are objective to the extent that we can apply labels to them, make analyses based upon the labels and come to conclusions. Examples:

- What is the meter of the music?
- What voices are performing the music?
- What instrument is playing?
- Who is the composer of this music?

Second, there are questions that call for statements of opinion or no system questions. In no system questions the answer is given in accordance with the person's subjective preference, there is no "right" or "wrong" answer. Answers are as varied as there are human beings and we have no way of assessing the validity of the thinking. Examples could be:

- Who is your favorite composer?
- Who is your favorite Christian performer?
- Do you prefer Baroque-style music or Romantic-style music?
- Do you listen to rock music?
- Do you like Gregorian chant?

Third, there are questions that call for reasoned judgment or multiple system questions. Multiple system questions require reasoning with more than one arguable answer. Answers are better or worse, well reasoned or poorly reasoned, and the goal is to reach the best answer within a range of possibilities. Many questions in music fall under this category for musical elements cannot always be labeled definitively. Music questions requiring reasoning with more than one arguable answer are:

- What was/is the composer doing with sound?
- What part of him/herself is the composer expressing in the music?

71

- Why is one piece of music better than another?
- Why is one performance of music better than another?
- How does music affect human emotion and behavior?
- How important is music in society?
- Who should pay for music to be created and performed?
- Does music have anything to do with morality?
- Should music be censored?

The most important questions for developing the musically questioning mind are those that require reasoned judgment, but this does not exclude other kinds of questions. Facts and definitions, and sometimes personal preferences, are also required to make reasoned judgments.

The musically questioning mind cannot be developed without some means of ensuring both questions and answers meet the highest standards of thinking. Choir members can learn to ask questions that involve answers of more than one word or personal preference. Praise team members can learn to focus their questions in different directions and think about the relevance of their questions as well as their answers. People can learn to test the logicalness of their answers so their thinking can be sustained and extended.

Criteria for evaluating music must go beyond peoples' personal preference. Their criteria need to be better or worse, well reasoned or poorly reasoned, and the goal is to help them arrive at personal criteria that are the best within a range of possibilities and within the limits of their musical background.

I believe you can help people in the music program of your church to develop musically questioning minds that will enable them to grow in their understanding and use of musical elements. First, you must think reasonably and reflectively about music yourself. Then you can help people think reflectively and reasonably about music. You can help people develop personal criteria for evaluating music compositions and performances. You can help people ask questions that assess the quality of musical thinking that is being done.

A PRACTICAL APPLICATION

Let me give you one practical example of how all of this fits together. I would not suggest you use every rehearsal to teach people how to read music. What I suggest is that you analyze the music you want to use with any of your groups and ask some of these same questions about that music. Reading music and performing at a higher level is the ultimate outcome.

At one time we could safely assume that most people in a church music organization would have a certain familiarity with the staff and notation. That may no longer be true. That means the worship leader has responsibility for helping others gain at least an elementary ability to read music. All of your music organizations will have members who have music reading problems. These problems should be attacked with patience and understanding, using actual music and not exercises. There is no longer any excuse for the rote memorization of a part.

I will use a singing group, either a choir or a praise team, to illustrate how people can learn to read music at an elementary level. The basic music reading problems are the relation of words to rhythm, and pitches; hearing and reading a voice part; having a sense of melodic and harmonic direction; and general musical understandings, such as dynamics and tempi. When singing contemporary praise songs or anthems there are added problems of syncopation.

First, we can help them gain an awareness of basic tonality. Use a simple song they all know, such as *America*.

- Diagram the tonic, sub-dominant, and dominant triads on a blackboard or overhead projector in treble and bass clefs. The bass voice outlines triads in measures 3, 6, and 8.
- Sing unwritten notes that are not a part of the triadic harmony, such as in the soprano and alto parts in measures 2 and 7.
- Analyze voice parts in relation to other parts, such as recognizing thirds, unisons, octaves, and other intervals between soprano and alto and tenor and bass primarily, but could be expanded to include all relationships between parts. The alto and soprano have parallel thirds in every measure of *America* except measures 1, 5, 6 and 7.

Second, we can help them learn the function of flats, sharps and naturals. Sing *America* as written, and then alter a note here and there with a flat or sharp so they have to alter the pitch when singing.

Third, we can develop rhythmic awareness by scanning texts in rhythm. For the person who does not read music, trying to sing words, intervals and rhythm at the same time is difficult. In some music it is difficult even for those who do read music. Use other vocal devices to teach rhythm, such as:

- Read rhythms as "one-and, two-and", "one-trip-let, two-trip-let" and "one-uh-and-uh, two-uh-and-uh."

- Isolate rhythmic groups that constitute one beat. This is easier when beams are connected. In some vocal music there are no beams and each note stands alone, and that makes it more difficult to see rhythmic groups by beat.

- Underscore the melodic shape of a rhythmic passage. I have always told singers to treat their voice part as if it were the melody. Otherwise they sing one note at a time with little awareness of the phrasing or melodic shape of the rhythm.

As the conductor you should know the music well enough to anticipate reading problems, but not to announce them in advance. Telling your singers there is a problem is a sure way of creating a problem! There are things you can do to make the initial reading of a new song more satisfactory.

- Establish the tonality and the main chords used.

- Identify the pulse unit, especially if it differs from the meter.

- Have the singers look for triads or near triads spelled out in a part.

- Isolate unisons, and other intervals to "tune up" on.

- Scan the words rhythmically.

- Sound pitch and try reading at tempo, stopping only to reestablish pitch.

- Correct the most glaring errors in pitch or rhythm. Time spent at this stage will eliminate much "drill" perhaps later.

- If anticipated problems didn't arise, they may later. Also, some non-anticipated problems may have arisen. Treat them accordingly.

- At subsequent readings, reinforce the sense of tonality and other factors of the first reading. Isolate melodic contour, rhythm patterns, and accidentals.

All this has been done (we hope!) with no mention of specifics that are generally thought of as being essential to music reading, *i.e.* names of notes, key signatures, time signatures, *et al*. With patience and understanding, your vocal groups can be led into better music reading as a part of greater musical understanding and better performance. Music groups being able to read music gives you more time in rehearsal to have the music prepared, interpreted and performed at a higher level.

CHAPTER SUMMARY

Much more could and should be considered, but that would go beyond the intentions of this chapter. Our purpose has been merely to give an overview of how you can function as a music teacher. We have seen that:

- A primary task of the worship leader is to develop the music skills, knowledge, and understandings of church members.

- People learn music in two ways. First, we have to have some basic skills to perceive sound as music. Second, everyone learns by thinking reflectively and reasonably about music.

- Perception is the gaining of knowledge directly through the senses. To perceive music is to see, hear, and feel melody, harmony, rhythm, form, and expression in music.

- The perception of music can be guided by having learners engage in certain behaviors from which we can infer that learning has taken place.

- Learning is growth, and all growth can be developed and guided. Teaching is a process of guiding development so growth takes place.

- Music has a logic that enables us to think about it reflectively. The trained musician thinks in terms of the logic of music, either consciously or unconsciously.

- The logic of music includes reasoning, a purpose, a point of view, concepts or ideas, some issue or question or problem, information, conclusions, assumptions, and implications.

- If anyone in the church is to learn by thinking, worship leaders need to ask questions that require people to think more broadly and deeply about the music information they receive, the music they hear and their emotional interactions with music.

- The process of learning music skills follows the sequence of receiving a model of the total skill required; receiving a model of each separate act involved in the total skill; identifying the separate acts to be performed in their sequence; exploring each separate act and the total skill through practice guided by the teacher; receiving immediate corrective feedback from the teacher during practice; and having adequate repetitive practice with enough duration to develop habitual performance with enough frequency that the skill is not lost.

CHAPTER 7

YOU ARE A LEADER OF WORSHIP

One of the main tasks of the worship leader is to lead in public, corporate worship. Literature is available which deals with the mechanics of this leadership, but too often the mechanics get in the way of understanding what we are about as worship leaders. In order to be an effective worship leader, we must come to some conclusions about what worship is and what worship means; the function of music in worship, including choirs, praise teams and congregational song; and music in relation to rites of passage. The emphasis in this chapter will not be so much on the "how" of leadership in worship, but on the "why" of leadership in worship.

WHAT IS WORSHIP?

While on the faculty of the New Orleans Baptist Theological Seminary, I was part of a team that taught a required course in worship leadership. Each year some three hundred students were asked to give their definition of worship for the first class assignment. There were as many definitions as there were students, which indicates the difficulty in defining what all of us are involved with regularly.

Our word "worship" comes from two Middle English words, *weorth* and *scipe*. *Weorth* is our word "worth" and means "worthiness and honor." When applied to people it means a person has a quality that commands esteem or respect. *Scipe* is an early form of our word "ship". When used as a suffix, as it is in worship, it means a state of being. This word was in common use when the King James Bible translators did their work, so certain Hebrew and Greek words were translated as worship, meaning God has a quality of being that we recognize and so give Him our esteem and respect.

The principal Old Testament word is *shachah*, that means "bow down," "kneeling before", and "prostrate oneself". The idea is the reverential attitude of mind or body or both, combined with attitudes of religions adoration, obedience, and service.

The principal New Testament words are *proskuneo*, "kiss (the hand or the ground) toward," in the oriental fashion of bowing prostrate upon the ground, and *latreuo* that means "to serve." The translators of the Septuagint, the Greek Old Testament used in Jesus' time, equated the Greek *proskuneo* with the Hebrew *shachah*.

These biblical words indicate that our worship should involve reverence before God and service for God. If we truly worship God we will serve Him. We could think of worship as God's revelation in Jesus Christ and our response to that revelation in awe, reverence and obedient service. The pivotal point of this definition is Christ. It is this center that distinguishes Christian worship from all other worship.

What does our worship say about God? What does our worship say about our response to God and His revelation in Christ? What does our worship say about our participation in the body of Christ, about our priesthood as believers, about our commitment to the work of Christ in the world? If worship is the response of man to God's revelation in Jesus Christ, then we need to think both about the nature of God's revelation and the ways we should respond to it. Instead of thinking about what people want, we should think about what God wants in worship.

The question is often raised whether worship should honor God or edify believers. If we honor God it means we give him the respect and esteem He deserves because of who He is. If believers are edified they have received instruction that encourages them toward intellectual, moral, and spiritual improvement.

The question is not really either/or, but both/and. God is honored when believers are edified, and believers are edified when God is honored. Worship is ascribing worth to God, and what better way of ascribing worth to Him than in the changed lives of those who worship God? Our worship needs to express the faith system both of the man in the pew and the man in the pulpit. Our initial response to God's revelation in Christ is through conversion, but believers are expected to grow in this experience. This is what edification is all about. Can people worship God in spirit and in truth until they have grown in their religious experience?

Worship is primarily a one-to-one relationship with God, and that relationship can find expression in private, small group, or body worship. Worship within the body of the fellowship on Sunday has a greater element of risk than worship privately or in a small group, for we are more open to the exposure of our sins and human frailties in the larger fellowship.

Consequently, we will discover people have a natural resistance to anything in worship that threatens their security. Psychotherapists are familiar with resistance in their clients, and this usually indicates the therapist is getting close to areas of personality that need help. We should view this natural resistance to change and innovation in worship in the same way.

There are some things that are common to all worship whether private, small group, or congregational. These are praise, prayer, confession, commitment, intercession, Scripture, and similar items. However, there are two other elements in Christian worship that are common and are frequently misunderstood: liturgy and ritual.

LITURGY

The evangelical Christian will often pour scorn on what he calls "liturgical services," in contrast to more spontaneous worship. However, this is a false distinction. There is not a contrast between liturgical and non-liturgical worship; the contrast is between liturgical worship and open worship.

The word liturgy comes from the Greek word *leitourgia*, which means a burdensome public office that the richer Athenian citizens discharged at their own expense. This was a service to the community. A *leitourgos* was one who was paid by the wealthy citizen to perform this service in his stead. Literally, then, a liturgy is a work or service of the people. In modern terms, we could think of the ordering of worship as a liturgy, the things the people do when they worship. Likewise, if we think of a worship order as a "service" it should be a reference to what people do before God when they worship.

We can make a distinction between a fixed liturgy and a free liturgy, for most churches have an order to worship. A fixed liturgy is one that is prescribed by the denomination, and there may be several alternates to choose from. However, in order to have properly sanctioned worship, a local church must use one of the prescribed orders.

In the fixed liturgy even the words to be used for such items as calls to worship, collects, prayers, and Scripture readings are prescribed. The same order and the same words are used each week, with some variation permitted for the seasons of the year, such as Christmas and Easter.

In the free liturgy, responsibility for order in worship is the responsibility of the leaders in each local church. Nothing is prescribed by the denomination, and the local church need follow no particular order to meet denominational approval. There may be set prayers and collects, but local leadership prepares these.

Open worship, on the other hand, has no order at all except that which occurs spontaneously. The extreme form of open worship would be that of the Quakers and some charismatic house churches.

It has been my practice to have a fixed liturgy with opportunities for open worship incorporated into it. In order for us to keep spontaneity, we used several liturgies, rotating every month or so. On Christmas morning there was open worship, the only thing planned being a short devotional message. Open worship consisted of open prayer from the congregation, personal testimonies, prayer requests, singing a favorite hymn, and even someone volunteering a vocal solo. In this way, the best of both liturgical and open worship was preserved.

RITUAL

Like liturgy, there are those who heap scorn on what they call "ritualistic worship." However, those who disdain ritual the most still have ritual in their worship. A ritual is a formal ceremony that is repetitious. The rite incorporates gestures, words, sacred objects, and postures. The two most common rituals are baptism and the Lord's Supper. These two rites are very repetitious, for there is not much that can be changed in the way they are performed.

The problem is not one of ritual versus no ritual. The problem is to preserve spontaneity in ritual so the rites do not become ends in themselves. Even the invitation at the close of an evangelistic sermon is a ritual that can easily become an end in itself.

THE MEANING OF WORSHIP

What is the difference between a definition of worship and the meaning of worship? At first the two terms seem to mean the same thing. However, a definition is a description of what is or what should be. The word "meaning" implies both value and definition. The meaning of worship lies in the values worship has for us. The meaning of worship defies precise definition since it is relative to the person. When people are asked to define worship, they usually do so in terms of its value to them.

The meaning of worship has importance for the worship leader since a definition of worship gives us no basis for the use of music. Worship can take place without any music at all, so, what is the value of music for the one who worships? Only when we answer this question can we have an intelligent approach to planning worship music.

First, we look at the value of worship in terms of human needs. Then we look at the function of music in worship as a partial means of meeting those needs.

HUMAN NEEDS MET IN WORSHIP

Psychologists think in terms of human needs that must be met if the person is to function properly as a person. Many of these needs are not pertinent to worship, and even some of the needs that can be met through worship are not pertinent to music. Those needs which worship music can help meet are autonomy and affiliation, participation, and verbalization and symbolization.

Autonomy and affiliation. Man has the need both for personal autonomy and affiliation with others. We want to be ourselves, but we also want to belong. Music is relevant to this need in that it could help to sensitize the person's awareness of God within him and around him, and at the same time provide a context of fellowship in which the urge for affiliation with others could find expression. Music is individualizing in that the person is free to find his own value and significance in what he does musically. Music is affiliating in that the person can become involved musically with others.

Participation. Related to the need to belong is the need to participate. Though modern man is characterized as a spectator rather than a participator, the need is still there. Singing hymns and contemporary praise songs is one way in which the worshiper can participate in worship. In order to participate effectively, the person needs to understand the service and his role as a participator. This would require some knowledge of how to sing and of the religious concepts expressed in the texts of hymns and songs, as well as the significance to him of purely instrumental music used in a service.

Participation involves expression of oneself. One of the tenets of Protestantism is the priesthood of believers in Christ. This means the Christian is solely responsible to God. Music can provide the opportunity for one to exercise this priesthood. People may express themselves freely as they sing or listen to an anthem or an organ prelude. The choir may convey meaning through its music in such a manner that people in the congregation are aware of feelings and ideas they cannot express, but wish to express.

Verbalization and symbolization. The need to verbalize and symbolize could also be met through congregational singing, and this is something every person has potential for. The texts sung should provide vocabulary for the individual to use in the personal expressions of faith. To verbalize about non-textual music is more difficult, but what we have considered in the chapter on philosophy should enable us to see the possibilities of this happening.

THE FUNCTION OF MUSIC IN WORSHIP

The worship leadership of a church may face a dilemma, for music can function either as an end in itself or as a means to an end. Many serious musicians object to any idea that music can be a "tool" to be used in attaining some nonmusical end, such as worship. The dilemma is intensified when we list the ways in which music functions in worship, for these are usually listings of nonmusical end results.

The primary function of music in worship is to meet human spiritual needs through the intensification of religious experience and as an edifying force. Music functions in worship through congregational music, choirs, praise teams and instruments. We also need to consider when music does not function properly in worship.

INTENSIFICATION OF RELIGIOUS EXPERIENCE

Music can intensify or make more vivid the total personal and corporate religious experience in worship. This is accomplished by adding a quality to worship. Music is a valuable part of human experience because it adds a quality to human existence. We have music and the other arts because they "humanize" us. In a technological society there is an even greater need for the humanities, for humans are in danger of becoming alienated from a life of feeling. The quality which music adds to worship is by stimulating the feeling side of people.

Music can unify corporate experience. When Christians come to worship, they come with many different and isolated ideas, feelings, and emotions. Music can be helpful in coordinating and unifying those ideas, feelings, and emotions, and directing them toward a corporate idea, feeling, or emotion. We are faced with the necessity of selecting music that will function in this way. The same overly familiar music used again and again, may not be effective in unifying a congregation. The same may be true of newer, unfamiliar music. We should strive for both the familiar and the new to be kept in balance in a service, hoping the new will become familiar.

Music can create a desired mood. Related to music as a unifying force is the function of music in creating a mood in worship. What moods do we desire in worship? Is there more than one mood desired on these occasions? Are there some moods that are undesirable? A healthy religious experience should enable people to reorient themselves to society and to God in a more meaningful way. The neurotic religious experience results in people retreating into their inner selves.

Any mood produced by music in worship which causes the person to withdraw into self, such as moods of sentimentality and nostalgia, would be undesirable as regular Sunday-by-Sunday fare. On the other hand, moods of reverence, praise, prayerfulness, assurance, confession, and commitment are moods to be desired each Sunday, since they direct us beyond ourselves. Both music and texts should influence positive Christian experience and not the neurotic withdrawal from real life.

Music can provide for participation. The church needs participants in order to exist, and people need to participate in the worship of the church in order to realize their full Christian responsibility and potential. The participation of church members in worship varies widely, but music can provide a means for everyone to participate. Not everyone can lead in public prayer or take overt participation in worship. Not everyone can use their singing voice in a choir or play an instrument. Still, music can provide an opportunity for participation through listening to music, reading hymn texts while they are being sung, and responding to music both physically and emotionally.

The genius of participation through music is the freedom given to each person to respond both to the music and through the music. One can pray inwardly through music without having to be concerned with grammar or with what his neighbor thinks about what he is saying. One can perceive God and religious truths through music in a way that is not dependent upon language, creed, or theological formulation for value and significance. While we can use music to create a general mood, there is no limit to the depth we can take that mood in our religious experience as we personally participate in and through music.

Music is valued because of its expressive nature. We like music that expresses something to us. We like music that enables us to express something through it. Religious experiences can be expressed both by the person and to the person through music. If a church is concerned with the spiritual growth of persons, then it seems logical that a church should also be concerned with the way that growth is expressed, both artistically and non-artistically, both verbally and nonverbally. If a church is concerned with people and their development of adequate theological expressions of faith through worship, then it seems logical for a church to be equally concerned with the development of adequate artistic expressions of faith through worship.

Worship music can aid in attempts to symbolize one's religious experience. The value of music in this process lies in the fact that music is not dependent upon a spoken or written language for its ultimate meaning. We do respond to music in linguistic expressions, but the value and significance of music goes beyond our ability and capacity to construct descriptive sentences to describe what music means to us.

Religious concepts come after religious experience. Salvation does not come through the formulation of concepts and logical structures, but through the experience of God's grace in repentance and faith. The concepts and logical structures are the results of religious experience. Through music we can go beyond the level of logical constructs to the level of basic religious experience. Even when language and logical constructs are involved in the texts set to music those religious concepts can be experienced.

AN EDIFYING FORCE

Music is a potent edifying force, as the advertising industry has discovered. Music can also be an edifying force in worship. Ideas can be implanted in the mind, the dramatic action of worship can be sensed, and an atmosphere of response to God can be created through music.

Music in worship may have meaning for us in that we value the emotional and intellectual responses music produces within us. Music in worship may have meaning for us in that music signifies something extra-musical to us, such as the conditions and qualities of our inner selves. The genius of music is the freedom music gives to each person to respond in his own way.

Our selection of worship music must be based upon its value as an enhancement of religious experience and as an edifying force. Ideally, we could hope that our selection of music would function as both. In order for music to function in these ways, we should examine all aspects of our worship music and discover how and why it is now functioning, and whether that function is a proper one.

This point is raised because music is an artistic medium that should be respected for what it is and for the human resources needed to create and perform music. To use music only to cover the noise of an assembling congregation, or to get the ushers down the aisle to take the offering, or to give the congregation a "seventh-inning stretch" does not seem to be a serious consideration of the power of music in worship.

Music in worship requires the same seriousness of purpose in its selection, preparation, and presentation as does the sermon. The ability of music to help meet human spiritual needs is dependent upon the musical sensitivity both of the congregation and the worship leadership. This indicates there are both musical ends and spiritual ends toward which we should aim.

Additionally, we should remember that some people need liturgical worship; others need open worship. Some need very familiar music; others need what is new. Some have great musical sensitivity, others very little. Some find great value and significance in music, others little at all. Most people need some of all these in any one worship service. The meaning of worship to the person in the pew is determined by his ability to find value and significance in what takes place in worship. Music has a part to play in this discovery.

CONGREGATIONAL SONG IN WORSHIP

We have mentioned congregational singing briefly before, but we need to think about the question: Why do we sing hymns and praise songs rather than read the texts in unison? There are three possible answers.

First, the texts are given an emotional or affective quality when set to music that the words alone do not possess. This consideration demands that a worthy text be set to worthy music. The text and the music should be able to stand alone as good examples both of literature and of music.

Second, singing is a force that draws a congregation together individually and corporately. Even groups that are of different theological persuasions can be drawn together by the same hymn or praise song. The religious convictions of the worshipers are expressed primarily as an offering of joy and praise to the Lord. At the same time, expression of faith is given to others outside the church. This means the congregation must understand what is being sung and must learn new hymns and songs that create deeper and broader expressions of conviction.

Third, singing is valuable in concept development. We do not learn unless we are personally involved in what is being learned, and unless involvement employs the affections of the deepest dimensions of personality. Singing is one of the activities in which we can become most personally involved in concept development. Therefore, the importance of learning new hymn and songs by children's and youth choirs cannot be minimized. Both children and adults have their religious concepts reinforced through singing.

THE CHOIR AND PRAISE TEAM IN WORSHIP

It is not important whether a church has a choir or praise team with ten or one hundred members, or a music budget of five or five thousand dollars. What is important is that a congregation understands the purpose of these singing groups and formulates correct attitudes about it. Needless to say, the choir and praise team members must also understand their purpose as a singing group. We can look at their function in three ways: as an extension of the congregation, as an opportunity for Christian service, and as an aid in developing worship skills.

An extension of the congregation. If the choir and praise team are an extension of the congregation, members of the congregation must be able to identify with them. The individual Christian must identify with individual choir and team members as well as the total choir and team membership. If a choir or praise team member exhibits a quality of life or attitude that is objectionable to a large segment of the congregation, his or her presence in the group can hinder its effectiveness. The individual Christian should be able to have the choir and praise team articulate ideas and feelings he or she cannot articulate. If the choir and praise team sing only music that is either above or below the musical-theological level of the people in the congregation, personal identification may not take place.

As an extension of the congregation, the church choir and praise team sing *to* the congregation, *for* the congregation, and *with* the congregation as they lead in congregational singing. The choir communicates musical and religious ideas to the worshiper through all types of non-congregational music. By singing portions of the service that the congregation is unable to do quite so effectively, the choir communicates for the people. If the music of the choir eliminates a portion of the congregation's opportunity for verbalization and symbolization through music, then we should reevaluate the role of the choir.

In order for these singing groups to communicate effectively, the congregation must be able to identify with the musical and religious ideas expressed in the choral music. The congregation must feel that the singers are not merely presenting a concert for the display individually and collectively of their musical abilities.

An opportunity for Christian service. Both the church choir and the praise team contribute to corporate worship at a musical level not otherwise possible to the congregation. This is because of the special musical gifts of choir and team members and the development of those gifts through training. These singers give freely of their gifts and talents as their service to God. It is this spirit of Christian commitment that enables a choir or praise team to provide a high level of worship leadership. The extent to which that leadership is given depends upon the degree to which the singers have the proper attitude of service and dedication.

An aid in developing worship skills. The church choir and praise team can assist the pastor in the development of congregational worship skills. This function begins with the singer's first visible or audible appearance in the service and continues as long as they can be heard or seen by the congregation. The choir and praise team must be with the pastor in all that is said and done. Though the choir and praise team are seen, they are not the focus of worship.

Apart from exemplifying an attitude of worship as they lead worship, the choir and praise team can aid in the development of congregational song. Few congregations pay enough attention to texts so they can sing the phrases with intelligibility. Since a musical phrase may pause or stop when the textual phrase must continue, the average worshiper will breathe with the musical phrase rather than the textual phrase. By careful planning and rehearsal, the choir and praise team can learn to breathe at the end of textual phrases so as to better help the congregation to sing the texts with new meaning.

INSTRUMENTS IN WORSHIP

Traditionally the organ has been the primary and sometimes sole instrument to accompany singing in worship. Today that accompaniment has been extended to include orchestras and praise bands. Unfortunately, some churches have silenced the organ and rely entirely on praise bands.

Some music is appropriate for an organ that is not as appropriate for any other instrument. This is also true of praise bands. It is not a question of eliminating any particular type of instrumental music, but using the instruments that are appropriate for the worship style of a church and for the style of a particular congregational song. It is possible that both an organ and a praise band would be appropriate for the same service.

What was said about choirs and praise teams would also apply to instrumental groups. Instrumental groups should be an extension of the congregation. They provide opportunities for Christian service and they are a great aid in the development of worship skills.

WHEN MUSIC DOES NOT FUNCTION PROPERLY

While worship music is valuable to most people most of the time, we need to understand how music can also stunt religious experience, disrupt corporate experience, produce negative moods and stifle participation. Music may be a negative edifying force as well as a positive one. Music does not function properly:

- When the people up front are performing rather than leading worship. Some churches have begun to use strobe lights and smoke machines to create "atmosphere" in worship. Whenever we draw attention to what

87

we are doing, and to ourselves, we are not leading worship. Whenever contemporary worship resembles a secular rock concert, we are not leading in worship.

- When it is too high to sing, especially for men. Often praise teams will present songs in keys that are easy for guitarists to play but are not easy for either men or women to sing.

- When the mood produced is an excessive romanticism. This is particularly true of men. I do not like singing contemporary Christian songs that have love song texts to Jesus, texts that are more appropriate for me to sing to my wife. Some of these have beautiful tunes, but you could be expressing love to the boy or girl next door as easily as expressing love for Christ. This is even more dysfunctional when the text does not even tell you to whom you are singing.

- When praise music is used exclusively in worship. The hymnbook has been discarded in many churches but they are still needed. People need songs to sing when they are hurting, struggling with illness, or facing death. Children and new believers need to have songs that help them articulate their faith. Both of these needs can be met through the singing of hymns.

- When the music is too loud. This has been one of the main objections to contemporary Christian music.

- When music is so rhythmically complex that the average person cannot sing it. This is a problem with some contemporary Christian music. Much of it was composed for a solo singer who has rhythmic freedom in performance, but this freedom cannot be successfully transferred to a congregation. Consequently, people stop trying to sing and just stand and listen as if at a concert instead of in worship.

- When technology gets in the way of worship. If a church projects text on a screen it is not effective for congregational singing if the words are not large enough to sing from. Projection is not effective if the person operating the projector or computer cannot make a smooth transition between verses.

WORSHIP AND RITES OF PASSAGE

Many of our religious rituals are called "rites of passage." These are those rituals that help us to find meaning as we experience changes in our personal status or roles. They reestablish equilibrium after crises of change, and they communicate to future generations what the community believes about change. Rites of passage have three phases: separation, transition, and reincorporation. Common rites of passage are birth and death, divorce, marriage, children leaving home and retirement. You may have worshipers on Sunday morning that are experiencing one or more of these phases in their personal rite of passage.

Music has an important function in four rites of passage that may be either a part of a regular worship service or complete services in themselves: baptism, the Lord's Supper, funerals, and weddings. I am giving you an interpretation of these rites of passage so you can have a better idea of what music is appropriate for each one.

BAPTISM

Too often baptism in the Evangelical Church tradition is an addendum to a regular service of worship. This leads to little planning to make this a significant event in the life of those being baptized and in the life of the church that is baptizing. If we are to plan music for this rite of passage, we need to think about what is taking place in baptism. We need to know what our music is enhancing, and for what and for whom music is an edifying force at a baptismal service. In churches with a fixed liturgy baptism may occur during worship or privately.

Baptism is a celebration of personal identity. Baptism, whatever its mode, is the way we experience and celebrate our personal identity as Christians and members of Christ's body. God has always made Himself known to man through visible means. We do not make it happen, for God gives of Himself as He chooses through His grace. Baptism calls forth a response from the believer, but it is always a response to the prior saving activity of God.

Baptism is a communal experience. The self-giving of God through baptism is a communal experience. Jesus did not merely proclaim a new message; He came to create a new community of faith, a people of His own. Baptism is an action done to us and not by us. It is the visible body of Christ manifested in a local fellowship of believers that does the baptizing, and it is to this fellowship we are joined. Since the local fellowship is a manifestation of the total body of Christ, we are joined to an organism that goes beyond the local fellowship. This is the primary reason baptism in most Evangelical churches is not administered privately without the presence of the worshiping community. As a celebration of our personal identification with Christ and His body, the identity it confers is structured by and derived from the community of faith.

Baptism is a celebration of community identity. As an act of the community of faith, baptism celebrates the identity of the community. It is a proclamation of what kind of community we are, to whom we belong, and what we are commissioned to do in the world. God makes His claim upon the church, and the church makes its claim upon those newly baptized. This is the meaning of body-life.

Baptism is a reminder of our identity. The church is always in need of remembering who and what it is as the body of Christ. We remember what we experience, and baptism is a touched, felt, and acted experience. The rite should enable the congregation to renew its experience and identity with others as followers of Jesus.

Since the worship leader is not usually the one who administers baptism on behalf of the church, you may have given little thought to your role in the rite. Your role is primarily that of planning and preparing appropriate music for the service, but you also have a personal responsibility for leading people to Christ and baptism, then in discipling them after baptism.

Let us be bold and strive for a worship service where the rite of baptism is central rather than an addendum. Baptism tells the world what the church believes about the new life in Christ and His community. Therefore, evangelism, commitment to Christ, and the fellowship of believers are all elements that need to be expressed musically. Unification of corporate experience, mood, congregational participation, expression of personal faith, and the symbolizing of faith are all elements in baptism that can be intensified through all types of music.

As an educational force, music can implant ideas in the mind about the necessity of the new birth and incorporation into the church. Music can help the congregation to sense the dramatic action of baptism and to create an atmosphere in which the self-giving of God can be perceived and responded to.

THE LORD'S SUPPER

As with baptism, the Lord's Supper too often is added at the end of a regular service of worship instead of being the central act of worship. If the worship leader is to lead worship centered round the Lord's Table, he must have some understanding of what is taking place when we observe the Lord's Supper.

The Supper evokes. A shared meal has always evoked feelings of unity and fellowship. In all cultures, eating and drinking together is a sign of love and oneness. The Lord's Supper is the means through which the risen Christ continually draws His people together and makes them one in Him.

The Lord's Supper calls forth our feelings about and consciousness both of Christ and our brothers and sisters who sit at table with us. The reality that is called forth is our fellowship with Christ and His people. The risen Christ is present with and in His people as they assemble to eat and drink with Him.

The Supper expresses. The Lord's Supper expresses the quality of the Christian community. The church is not a group of isolated individuals, but a gathering of those who have been called by Christ to be His own. The Lord's Supper gives a visible expression of our meeting and relating to one another. We do not express abstract ideas and concepts. Instead, we express the ideals of the Christian life and through the rite attempt to embody these ideals in the hearts, minds, and behavior of people.

The Supper invites. The Lord's Supper is an invitation to community. When we meet together we try to act as if we are not strangers, but brothers and sisters in Christ. We are invited to project our dreams and hopes for better Christian living into the ritual. We are invited to experience both the presence of Christ with us and our unity with Him and one another. We are invited to reconcile our differences and share together.

The Supper proclaims. As we eat and drink together, we proclaim the death of Christ for our sins. We proclaim the presence in the here and now of the risen Savior, and we proclaim His coming again in the future. We proclaim our individual participation in the benefits of Christ's death when we eat the bread. We proclaim our allegiance to Him and our continuing participation in the community of faith as we drink the wine. Just as Christ took ordinary bread and wine and made them extraordinary, we proclaim that Christ has taken us who are ordinary and made us extraordinary through His Spirit.

As with baptism, the worship leader does not usually preside over the Lord's Supper. Let us again be bold and plead for a service where the Lord's Supper is central to worship and not an appendage to a service. The action of the service would proceed in this direction: gathering as the church, praise, self examination and confession, commitment to Christ and His body through the sharing of the bread and cup, sharing the concerns of the community of faith, intercession and petition on behalf of the church and world; and scattering as the church to live and serve our fellowmen in Christ's name.

The dramatic action given above involves the formation of community and the service of the community to the world. Perhaps in no other service of worship can music, as an enhancement of religious experience and as an educational force, be utilized as fully as in the Lord's Supper. This is as it should be, for it is through this rite that the Christian community finds full expression.

THE CHRISTIAN FUNERAL

Through the funeral service, the church is saying what it believes about death and the hereafter. Everything in the service should point to the values the Christian community holds and uses to interpret the meaning of death. Too often, we have personalized the funeral to such an extent that the witness of the church has been lost.

The funeral should be personalized to a certain extent, but we must remember that it is primarily a service of worship. The funeral provides opportunity for the church to affirm the reality of death and grief; and in the midst of death and grief we can also affirm our continuing lives. While we give witness to the Christian view of death, a funeral, in my view (which some may disagree with) is neither the time nor place for an evangelistic appeal.

The fact that the funeral is a service of worship does not mean that those who are bereaved are neglected. The service should allow the bereaved to own their grief and to work through it. The worship of God should help the family accept all their bewildering feelings and get in touch with that part of themselves that God already knows.

For the church, a funeral service is an opportunity for church members to work out any unfinished grief from the past and to struggle in preparation for their own death in the future. Church members can affirm the feelings of the grief-stricken family and give them support as the community of faith. The feelings experienced should be owned and expressed and not manipulated or prescribed by the community.

For the worship leader, the funeral provides an opportunity to minister in a very meaningful way. Instead of sentimental and nostalgic songs, let us sing hymns of aspiration and faith! Imagine a grieving family struggling to its feet and singing "How Firm a Foundation" or "A Mighty Fortress Is Our God" along with fellow believers as an affirmation of faith. Some of the other moods we should want to express are those of hope, praise, and assurance.

In thinking about a funeral service, remember that the bereaved experience separation. They have lost one they love. While in the grief process they are in a state of transition. However, in six months or so they will be entering the process of reincorporation, and this gives us an added opportunity for ministry. Through personal ministry – such as lending them tapes and CDs, or through the music ministry – such as enlisting or reenlisting them in a choir, the worship leader can reach out to those who need to be reincorporated into the continuing life of the church.

THE CHRISTIAN MARRIAGE

The wedding ceremony is also an act of Christian worship. It is not a private affair between two people only. A man and a woman commit themselves to a lifelong covenant of companionship and call upon the church and God to be witnesses of the event. The wedding ceremony tells what the church believes about the permanent and deep relationship between a man and a woman. In the wedding ceremony the church attempts to assist the couple as they move from being single to being married.

The worship leader needs to examine the vows made and the entire structure of the service used by the pastor, for what is said reveals what it is all about. The ceremony tells us that love is an act of the will, not an emotion. The couple is asked if they will love one another, not if they do love one another. Consequently, any kind of popular song or art song that portrays love in a different vein should be questioned. Obviously the couple already loves one another or they would not be getting married.

The challenge is to define that love. It must be the mutual self-giving love of 1 Corinthians 13 that keeps married love from being only sentiment or sexual attraction. If couples choose their own songs without any guidance from you, they may select songs that emphasize the sentiment and sexual attraction rather than the self-giving.

A couple is God's gift to one another, so there is an element of joy in the service. There is commitment, there is permanence, and there is the blessing of God upon the couple. All these need musical expression. Above all, we are thinking of two Christian people being joined together. Somehow their basic faith in Christ must be brought to the forefront in the marriage ceremony as an act of worship. They give themselves in mutual submission to one another under the lordship of Christ, forgiving each other as Christ has forgiven them. Can this also find musical expression in a wedding?

The presentations of these rites of passage have been kept brief intentionally. It should be obvious that music can enhance the religious experiences of the rites, but what about music as an edifying force? It is not a question of teaching or not teaching; it is a question of what kind of teaching. Do we really teach what the church believes about the new life in Christ? Do we really teach what the church believes about the Christian community? Do we really teach what the church believes about death and the hereafter? Do we really teach what the church believes about the permanent and deep relationship of a man and a woman in marriage? Or do we believe one thing and teach another in the music we use in the observance of these rites?

PLANNING FOR WORSHIP

The worship leader may be responsible for planning the entire order of worship, or he may only select the hymns and other music used. Regardless, there must be joint planning by all those involved in worship leadership.

First, there should be an agreed liturgy or order of worship. Some churches have a different order each Sunday. Other churches have an order that is used for a period of time before changing to another one. Worship leaders and pastors need to discuss what variables are needed weekly in the order of worship, such as responses, prayers, readings, and music.

Second, worship should have a theme. It may be taken from the sermon topic, or from the sermon content. If the one preaching has developed an objective for the sermon in terms of congregational response, then this could be the theme. The congregational response is not always to an appeal to receive Christ. It might be a new attitude or a new way of living or a new commitment.

Third, once the theme is chosen, we must select worship materials that fit the theme. The materials should not only fit the theme; they must also be appropriate for the psychological flow of worship. One way of thinking about the flow of worship would be these moods, each following the other: gathering of the church, praise of God, confession and restitution, communing with God, hearing from God, responding to God, and scattering as the church to live and work in the world.

The theme chosen should not interfere with the flow of worship. If the sequence of moods given were used, it would be inappropriate to sing a hymn of praise during a time of confession and restitution or to have an offertory during communing with God. If the flow of worship is determined, there is a logical place for each element in the liturgy. For example, responding to God would include the invitation time, the offertory, and a litany of commitment.

Fourth, planning should be done far enough in advance that worship materials can be secured and properly prepared. Many preachers plan their sermons months in advance, following an overall theme, with each sermon a part of that theme. The church musician can plan his work in accordance with what the preacher has planned, for the choir and others will need ample time to practice and learn new music materials.

CHAPTER SUMMARY

In this chapter we have discussed several aspects of worship that relate to the work of the worship leader. The emphasis has not been so much on the "how" of worship leadership as the "why" of worship leadership. We have thought about the following:

- Worship is a person's response to God's revelation in Jesus Christ.

- Through worship, the church tells what it believes about God, about Christ, and how one can and should respond to God in Christ.

- All Christian worship contains both liturgy and ritual.

- The meaning of worship is the value it has for us in our spiritual development.

- There are certain human spiritual needs that worship helps to meet.

- The function of music in worship is the intensification of religious experience and as an edifying force.

- It is possible for music to be dysfunctional in worship.

- Congregational music is important because the texts are given an emotional quality they do not possess in themselves; singing hymns and praise songs draw a congregation together; and are an aid to religious concept development.

- The role of the choir and praise team is to sing *to* the people, *for* the people, and *with* the people.

- The choir and praise team are an extension of the congregation; they provide people with the opportunity for Christian service and aid in the development of worship skills.

- There are four rites of passage that may be complete worship services in themselves, or adjuncts to a regular worship service. Music is valuable as an intensification of religious experience and as an edifying force in these rites.

- In baptism the church tells what it believes about the new life in Christ and initiation into the community of faith.

- In the Lord's Supper the church tells what it believes about the quality of new life in the community of faith.

- In the funeral the church tells what it believes about death and the hereafter.

- In marriage ceremonies the church tells what it believes about the deep and permanent relationship of a man and a woman in marriage.

- Worship planning requires the cooperation of all concerned with worship leadership, and includes the agreement of the liturgy; selecting a theme for the worship service; choosing appropriate materials which follow the psychological flow of worship; and planning far enough in advance that proper materials can be secured and prepared.

CHAPTER 8

YOU AND A CHURCH

Your relationship with a church is very important to a successful ministry. In this chapter we want to think about some things that have more to do with your personality and your philosophy of life than with your training and experience in music; things that can affect the pastor–worship leader relationship and the church–worship leader relationship both positively and negatively. It is important to your emotional and spiritual well being that you raise these questions and receive answers you can live with before you join a church staff.

WHO EVALUATES YOUR WORSHIP LEADERSHIP?

Who will evaluate the quality of your worship leadership? Quality is a word we hear in connection with music and worship. Coupled with quality is an emphasis upon standards. There is the constant push in some churches to raise musical standards and to have quality worship. This is not limited only to traditional music and worship; there is the push to have quality contemporary music and worship, too. This desire for quality is not wrong in itself. The problem is that we simply do not know what we are talking about!

What is quality? What is excellence? What are standards? The dictionary says quality is a level or degree of excellence. Quality is a characteristic or something that a person or thing has which is special. What is a standard? Again, the dictionary reveals that a standard is a thing or a quality by which something can be measured or tested. A standard is the required level of quality or proficiency. The word excellence means very great merit or quality.

Frustrated? You should be. Quality is a standard of excellence. A standard is the required level of quality. Excellence is very great quality. What are we talking about? What would happen if our theology were defined in such an ambiguous fashion?

We can define what quality music and worship is for us, personally, but our definition says nothing about who determines that quality, the level of excellence to be expected, or how the quality of your work can be tested or measured.

Quality is a value, something we think is important in giving a meaning to life and making it more bearable. Quality relates to those things, those thoughts, those feelings, and those experiences that elevate man above the mere level of animals. Quality is that which we place at the top of our survival and life enhancement values. Quality is what we are prepared to spend our time and money for.

Who determines the quality of music and worship in a church? You? The pastor? The denomination? A music committee? A worship committee? If the pastor or a committee determines the quality of music and worship you must be sure that you are willing to accept their standards. You will not be called to impose your personal standards, likes, and dislikes upon a church.

If a pastor is the right kind of pastor, he wants the worship leader to know how to meet the spiritual needs of people through music and worship. To do this, you must help him to determine the quality needed, to consider the standards to be pursued, and how to evaluate your effectiveness.

Quality in music and worship can be defined only in relation to a particular group of people in a particular place at a particular time and for a particular purpose. God has always worked this way with His people. Quality will be that kind of music and worship a group of people think is of value in experiencing God and proclaiming the Christian message. Quality in music and worship is what your people place at the top of the list of values that help to sustain and to enhance the Christian life. Quality music and worship is what your people are willing to spend their time and money for. And do you know what? Their concept of quality may be totally different from yours.

WHAT LEVEL OF EXCELLENCE?

What level of excellence should be expected? A standard for excellence is elusive, but one we must strive for. There are some things we should do and some things we should not do in the pursuit of excellence. Do not compare apples with potatoes. Do not compare Bach with Gaither. Compare Bach with Bach and with other baroque composers. Compare Gaither with Gaither and with other contemporary gospel music writers. Do not even compare Bach with Beethoven if you are trying to determine which one is greater, for they come from different style periods. We can only state a personal preference, not objective fact.

Do not talk about "good" music, for this implies there must be "bad" music. The "good" is an ethical term, not a musical one. We need to think in terms of what is better than, and why this or that piece is better. This Bach piece is better than that Bach piece. Why? Because of its difficulty? Because of its accessibility to performer and listener? Because it is appropriate for the occasion? Why is this Gaither piece better than that Gaither piece? Our answers must lie in the realms of suitability for the occasion and its accessibility to performer and listener. Both Bach and Gaither could be suitable for the same occasion. One is not "good" and the other "bad."

Do not impose standards that are beyond the time and resources you have to reach them. If you do not have the personnel in your choir and the rehearsal time available that a professional choir has, then do not expect your choir to sound like professionals

Do justice to the music you use. Music has an internal integrity that must be respected. We should never get the notion that Handel requires seriousness of purpose, while gospel music does not. All kinds of music require seriousness, and you are dishonest without this attitude.

You must have as your standard of excellence the best your people can do. Not "the best" as an abstraction, but the best you and yours are capable of. Your people are capable of more than either you or they think possible. As you work together over a period of time, your standards change as capabilities change. A rigid expectation is doomed to failure.

You must know how your people want to articulate and to proclaim their message. I do not mean by this the kind of music they want. It is very possible that the music they like and want is inadequate to articulate and to proclaim their message, and they do not know it.

Likewise, if you come in and impose a different kind of music upon them, it could also be inadequate. Consequently, your task is to discover how your people want to give their message, then to help them discover many kinds of music that can become the means of expression. You may discover that country-Western style gospel music is as valid as Mendelssohn. You may discover that you can have both in the same worship service and no one thinks it strange.

HOW CAN QUALITY BE MEASURED?

How can we evaluate the quality of our music and worship? There are various means. We could depend upon the likes and dislikes of the pastor. The growth of choir membership could be a measure, as could the number of new hymns learned by the congregation. The growth of the adult choir in its ability to read music and sing more difficult anthems could be used.

How does the thoughtful pastor evaluate his preaching ministry? Not in attendance or giving or the number of programs or additions to the church. All of these things can be influenced by many factors other than preaching, and they can be manipulated.

The thoughtful pastor plans his preaching according to the spiritual needs of the people. Only they can measure their spiritual growth, and the pastor must devise a means of feedback from the people. The worship leader must make the same approach: plan to meet spiritual needs through music and receive evaluation through feedback from the people.

You need to discover what hymns and contemporary songs are the most meaningful and why. What kinds of instrumental music help them in worship and why? What direction should the music and worship take in future? What kinds of music do they desire in order to express their religious experiences? What religious experiences do they have which need to find musical expression? These and many other questions need to be raised with your church members.

This could involve a worship questionnaire. Some churches do not respond positively to questionnaires, so use your music and/or worship committee as a sounding board. This evaluation could occur any time and any place you can get a group together to talk and to listen. I would urge trying to have a talkback in the church fellowship hall following a choir program where there could be discussion of the program along with cups of coffee. All of these will help you to evaluate your music program.

TO WHOM ARE YOU RESPONSIBLE?

It is important to know to whom you are responsible. If a church is structured on a business model the pastor may function like a CEO with elders and/or deacons serving as a board of directors. You would be responsible to the pastor who would have the power to dismiss you.

In other church settings you might be responsible to a music committee, worship committee or personnel committee. They would be the ones to evaluate your work and have the power to dismiss you.

In a further setting you could be responsible to the church membership that would have the power to evaluate your work and dismiss you upon the advice of the pastor or a particular committee.

You will need to determine which setting fits your personality and way of working. However, despite the church structure, you must be able to work with the pastor. The pastor is responsible for the overall spiritual welfare and direction of the church. What you do or do not do will aid the pastor or hinder him. In most churches the pastor will have the final word on most issues, so be sure you can work with a pastor.

How is Worship Planned?

Some pastors have the mistaken notion that they cannot plan long range because that quenches the work of the Holy Spirit. I believe the Spirit can help plan for six months as easily as planning for one week. It is not usually the Spirit who is at fault.

Every pastor I have worked with as worship leader has planned his preaching only on a week–to–week basis. One pastor never knew until Saturday night what Sunday's sermon would be. After getting the sermon he was never sure what the conclusion would be. He expected me to choose the closing hymn on the basis of his conclusion. Imagine the agony of sitting there and trying to guess at his conclusion and think of an appropriate hymn!

Planning would enable you to select new music to fit topics. You would be able to locate film clips, or skits or readings that would be appropriate. Planning would give you the time needed to rehearse the music and select people for skits, readings and to preview film clips.

You must know and understand how a pastor plans or fails to plan. Some pastors who fail to plan can make difficult requests of a worship leader, expecting something that may be beyond your ability to provide. Your concept of planning must be compatible with that of the pastor if you are to work together successfully.

Are You Free to Complement the Sermon?

People today are visually oriented. While they will sit politely for a thirty-minute sermon, what is said will more likely stick in their memories when props or drama or similar stimuli accompany the sermon. The sermon time is still thirty minutes but the voice of the pastor may last only twenty minutes or less. As a worship leader you can help your pastor discover new ways to present his sermon material.

Preaching is important, and we should not diminish its importance, but worship is more than preaching just as worship is more than music. A pastor may be shocked whenever we dare suggest that worship is more than his sermon or that we can worship without a sermon. Some pastors think the sermon is worship and whatever comes before are merely preliminaries.

Many pastors are unaware that the sermon can include skits, readings, film clips and songs and that resources are available for them to do this. I once preached a sermon that included the point that we are reluctant to let go of our sins instead of cutting them loose. One scene from the film "The Mission" illustrated this beautifully in three minute, and said more in those three minutes than I could have said. In another sermon I wanted a quote from Alice in Wonderland and had two people read the parts as a skit while a picture of the scene from the book was shown.

Songs can also be used to illustrate a point. In a sermon on the spiritual fruit of kindness I used Glen Campbell's song *Take a Little Kindness*. I have used songs by U2 and Kansas among others. While the song is sung, the words are projected on the wall. The response has always been positive and comments from the congregation indicate the songs were effective.

Don't push this point. All sermon topics do not lend themselves to these additional features and the preparation required is extensive. You might find it difficult to do these things every week over an extended time unless you had adequate secretarial assistant. Talk with your pastor about varying the sermon for a one-time trial to see how you work together on it and how the congregation responds.

In this regard you need to know how much freedom you have in complementing the sermons of the pastor. At the same time you need to be willing to find and use materials the pastor may need. Both you and the pastor need to remember that finding worship materials, then preparing and rehearsing them takes time.

IS CHURCH GROWTH DEPENDENT UPON YOU?

I know of a church where the minister of music was shifted to another church staff position because the pastor was convinced the lack of attendance and church growth were caused by the music used in worship. An interim was employed to direct the choir and lead congregational singing.

Both with the former minister of music and the interim director, the order of worship began with a welcome song that was usually never sung by the congregation because it was "meet and greet time," prayer/scripture, a medley of praise songs, a film clip or ministry moment, a medley of praise songs, the choir selection, sermon, invitation, offertory, benediction, benediction song, and postlude. Words to hymns and praise songs were projected on a screen in front of the congregation. This never varied except for the occasional baptism or infant presentation. At the end of two years with this arrangement Sunday School attendance and worship attendance had continued to fall and no new members were joining the church.

Some churches think that eliminating the hymnbook and projecting words on a screen or wall will ensure growth. Or, that by singing with a praise band rather than an organ will help growth. Or, growth will come by singing only praise songs rather than hymns. If you ask them why they think this they have no real reason, except growing churches have these things. The question should be asked: *are there growing churches that do not do these things?*

Music may play a role in a church's decline or lack of growth, but other factors should also be considered. Merely firing a worship leader or singing praise songs with a praise band or projecting words on a screen is not a sure-fire way to have church growth. Church growth comes when individual Christians share their faith with neighbors and bring them to church.

Is There a Budget?

Some churches operate on a budget that is adopted by the church. In other churches the pastor may control the budget. Some churches still do not operate with a budget but make special appeals for donations to specific causes and needs.

You need to know if you will have funds available to do your work and how much control you have over your expenditures. Will you have adequate funds to buy worship materials? Will there be funds for you to have secretarial help? Will you have funds available to tune pianos and to replace instruments as they wear out? What is the process for planning the church budget? How much input do you have in the planning process? Will you have a housing allowance? Will you have a car allowance?

There are also some money matters that are important to you beyond church expenditures. A very important money issue is whether or not the church participates in a retirement program in addition to social security. Will you have sufficient funds at retirement?

If a pastor wants to make changes in worship style, it could cost money. Buying projection equipment, microphones, wall screens, electronic keyboards or synthesizers and computers will cost a large sum of money if quality equipment is bought. You can help your pastor by determining what equipment is needed and making cost analyses for him. How much input will you have in the final decision?

CONCLUSION

I hope the questions in this chapter help you to see the breadth of your work as a worship leader that go beyond what you do on Sunday. I hope, too, that the questions have alerted you to some important issues you need to have settled in your own mind before you join a church staff. My prayer will be for you to have a very blessed and rewarding position in worship leadership.

APPENDIX

FOR PERSONAL GROWTH

CHAPTER 1

1. On a sheet of paper, list your strengths and weaknesses side by side. Then, after thought and prayer, write a sentence beside each item on your lists that tells why you think it is a strength or weakness.

2. To own your feelings think about those things which bother you the most. Then make a series of sentences that describe what triggers the feeling and what the feeling is. Use this model: "When anyone (does or says this or that) I feel (angry, sad, happy, etc.)."

3. What feelings are you afraid of and want to hold in control? After some thought, make a list of those "dangerous" feelings. Then find a trusted friend to share them with in prayer.

4. Write a series of sentences that express for you what a minister should *be*, rather than what he should *do*. Share these thoughts with your friend.

5. What is your motivation for being a minister? Can you make a list of reasons why God is worthy of your service?

6. To gain a better self-image and confidence in your ability to respond positively to your emotions, you must feed positive thoughts into the unconscious part of your personality. To do this, try the following:

    a. Find a quiet place where you can read the Bible and pray.

    b. After reading and prayer, try to become totally relaxed with eyes closed.

    c. Concentrate on a word or a phrase, such as "Christ loves me," or concentrate on an object, like the cross.

    d. Let your mind focus entirely upon the one thought or object, asking God to fill you with His Spirit.

After many struggles in trying this, you can eventually discover a new presence of God and an awareness of His communicating with you. As the two of you communicate, give God those troublesome emotions and let Him take care of them for you.

7. Write out a personal mission statement. A mission statement for your worship ministry and one of the groups you work with, like the adult choir, praise band, etc. *Think about a personal mission statement for me.*

CHAPTER 2

Study a familiar piece of music used in worship and try to answer these questions about it:

1. Describe the music. What is its structural form? Its expressive form?

2. Is the music expressive apart from the text? What is your response to the music? How would you describe the music? How would you describe the feelings aroused by the music?

3. Is the text expressive apart from the music? What is your response to the text? How would you describe the text? How would you describe the feelings aroused by the text?

4. What is there about the music that arouses your feelings? Consider such items as tension-release, shape of the melody, rhythmic organization, and harmony used.

5. What is there about the text that arouses your feelings? Consider such items as biblical imagery, references to deity, and theological content.

6. What does the music symbolize for you as an artistic symbol and as a liturgical symbol?

7. What does the text symbolize for you as an artistic symbol and as a liturgical symbol?

CHAPTER 3

1. How do you determine what is "good" music?

2. Can music reveal God and/or religious truth? Why?

3. Must music be associated with worship in order to be "religious"? Why?

4. How would you determine if a piece of music was sacred or secular?

5. Can you justify an instrumental prelude in worship as you can an anthem, a hymn or a praise song? Why?

6. Think about a familiar praise song. What is the value of the music to you? How do you value it? Why do you value it?

7. Take an unfamiliar anthem and evaluate it for use in worship. What criteria do you use to make your decision? Why would you use it in worship? Why would you not?

8. Take both a hymn and a praise song that are unknown to you and evaluate them for use in worship. What criteria do you use to make your decision? Why would you use either or both in worship? Why would you not use either or both in worship?

CHAPTER 4

Think about these three questions; then write a short essay on each, giving your own conclusions:

1. What is the theological basis of worship music in your church? What should it be?

2. How does theology relate worship music to the total program of your church? How should it relate?

3. What theological criteria do you use for the evaluation of worship music? If you have no criteria, how would you go about establishing criteria?

CHAPTER 5

1. Study the cultural responses of your congregation. Is there a relation between those responses and the style or type of church music they prefer? Give reasons for your answer.

2. What effect does the "electronic church" have on the type of church music you can use?

3. What responsibility does the church have to preserve, advance, and continue music as an art? Give reasons for your answer.

4. What is the primary purpose of your church music program: musical, aesthetic, social, evangelistic, or worship? What basis is there for your determining this?

5. Take the conversionist response to culture, and justify it to an imaginary friend who holds each one of the other four responses.

2.25.21

CHAPTER 6

1. Select any music group you are responsible for. Think about what music skills they need. Select one skill and outline a procedure for teaching that skill using this format:

   - What is the model of the expected motor skill they need to learn?
   - What model of each separate act involved in the required skill will you use? [Remember the example of changing a tire?]
   - What are the separate acts in the skill to be performed? They are learned in what sequence? [Do you jack up the car first, or take off the wheel first?]
   - How will you guide their practice so they explore both each separate act and the total skill? [How do you tell them to jack up the car, remove the wheel, etc.?]
   - How will you give corrective feedback during practice?
   - How often and how long will they need repetitive practice to keep the skill from being lost? [How many tires do they need to change before they know how to do it?]

2. Select a song suitable for choir or praise team that you want them to learn. Analyze the song in terms of the music concepts and skills inherent in it. Isolate musical examples from the song that support your analysis. Make a list of questions you could ask that would help choir members think about the concepts and skills you want them to learn. Plan some rehearsal time for musical thinking, using the model above.

3. Think about melody. Then write as many concept statements of melody you can think of.

4. Make a rehearsal outline for teaching a new song to a choir or praise team using the ideas presented in this chapter.

CHAPTER 7

1. Think about a worship service that has been especially meaningful for you. What was its value to you, and what did it signify for you? What was its psychological flow? What was its theme? How did music intensify your experience, and how was it an educational force? What personal needs were met through the total worship experience?

2. Give some thought to the liturgy and ritual evident in the order of worship in your own church. Is there a good psychological flow? Is there a theme each Sunday? Are the musical portions of the service appropriate for where they occur? How could you improve upon it?

3. Think about each of the four rites of passage. Then make a list of hymns and other music you think would be appropriate to function as an intensification of religious experience and as an educational force in each rite.

4. Show how your choir, praise band and/or praise team are leading in worship rather than giving a concert.

CHAPTER 8

Answer the questions in this chapter in terms of your expectations of a position in worship leadership. Be as detailed as possible. Then answer these questions:

1. Which items are non-negotiable for you?
2. Which items are you willing to adjust to meet the needs of a church?
3. What are some additional things you would like to know about a church before you joined its staff?
4. How much stress can you take if your expectations are not met quickly?
5. How flexible do you think you really are?

After you have answered the questions, find a full-time worship leader who would be willing to discuss your expectations with you.

Biography

William Loyd Hooper

William Hooper attended Southwest Baptist College (now Southwest Baptist University) in Bolivar, Missouri, at that time a small two-year college. Following graduation, Hooper and his new wife served the First Baptist Church of Picher, Oklahoma as Minister of Music and Education.

Then, it was on to William Jewell College in Liberty, Missouri in 1953. While attending Jewell he had a student pastorate in Denver, Missouri. He received a Bachelor of Arts degree with a major in philosophy and was awarded the David Alan Duce Award in Philosophy at commencement exercises. Following graduation Hooper taught public school vocal and instrumental music, kindergarten through high school, for two years at Essex, Iowa.

Graduate studies followed at the University of Iowa where he earned a Master of Arts degree in music in 1956 with a concentration in voice. Hooper was awarded a graduate assistantship and was the librarian for the University Chorus.

The next four years were spent in Bolivar, Missouri as professor of voice at Southwest Baptist College, a small junior college. He directed the College Choir, trained both men and women quartets that were used in college recruitment, and organized a sixteen-voice College Chorale.

Doctoral study followed at George Peabody College of Vanderbilt University in Nashville, Tennessee. In 1956 he received the Ph.D. degree in music with a concentration in church music. While at Peabody he was a Jesse Jones Scholar and served the First Baptist Church in Old Hickory, Tennessee as part-time minister of music and education.

After his two years of doctoral candidacy were finished, Hooper went to The New Orleans Baptist Theological Seminary in 1962 as professor of music theory. Two years later he was promoted to Dean of the School of Church Music, a position he held until 1974. As Dean he played a leading role in getting the Seminary accredited by the Southern Association of Colleges and Schools and the School of Church Music accredited by the National Association of Schools of Music. Hooper also led the School of Church Music to begin a doctoral program in church music. While at the Seminary he was baritone soloist at St. Charles Avenue Baptist Church.

In the summer of 1969 Hooper and his family traveled to Zambia to work with churches there in training choirs. A year of sabbatical study began in the fall of 1969 in London, England. Hooper studied music composition privately with Humphrey Searle at the Royal College of Music. He returned to New Orleans in the fall of 1970.

Hooper has been a composer since high school days. He began composing by arranging charts for his dance band with Stan Kenton and Igor Stravinsky as his models. His first serious composition and performance came as a freshman at Southwest Baptist College with a piece for wind band titled "Daydream." It was also performed at Northwestern University under the title "Music for a Motion Picture."

Beginning in 1962 and continuing to the present, many choral compositions have been written and published by Concordia Press, Broadman Press, Carl Fischer and Word Music. Also in 1962, Hooper's first book, "Church Music in Transition" was published. The cantata "His Saving Grace Proclaim" was published and recorded in 1968.

In 1973 Le Petite Theatre du Vieux Careé in New Orleans asked Hooper to compose incidental music for their production of Anouhil's play "Becket." In 1973 he won the Delius Composition Competition and in 1974 he won the New Times Composition Competition.

A move was made back to England in 1974. Hooper was head of music at Newstead Wood School for Girls in the London Borough of Bromley for five years and served as worship pastor for Emmanuel Baptist Church in Gravesend, Kent. In 1979 the church called him as pastor. While serving as pastor he completed a year of study in psychotherapy at the Westminster Pastoral Care Foundation.

He and his family returned to the United States in 1983 to become Dean of the School of Fine Arts at Southwest Baptist University, retiring from that institution in 1998. Since retirement he has continued his ministry as Minister to Senior Adults at First Baptist Church, Bolivar, Missouri.

Major compositions have included "Jubilee", a cantata celebrating the 50th anniversary of New Orleans Baptist Theological Seminary (1968), "Canticle of Praise" (children's cantata, 1968), "The Vision of Nahum" (2001) and "By the Grace of God for Chorus and Instruments" (2002) to celebrate the 125th anniversary of Southwest Baptist University. In addition to "Church Music in Transition" Hooper has also written "Music Fundamentals" (1964), "Ministry and Musicians" (1982) and "Fundamentals of Music," 4 vols. (1986). Numerous other instrumental and keyboard pieces have been composed as well.

Hooper is married to the former Doris Jean Wallace and has two children, William, Jr. and Carol Ann Cooper, seven grandchildren, and one great grandchild.

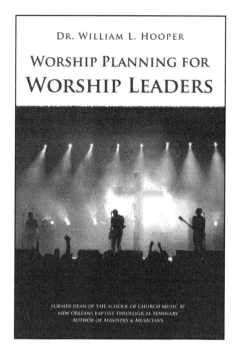

WORSHIP PLANNING FOR WORSHIP LEADERS

Dr. William L. Hooper

Introducing the **Worship Leadership Training Series** from Alexander Publishing. *Worship Planning for Worship Leaders* is the second in a series of practical problem/ solution training guides by Bill Hooper to help you have mighty Kingdom impact. Covers: *Worship is About God, Ordering Christian Worship, Role of the Worship Leader, Planning for Worship, Planning for Worship Ensembles, Planning for Congregational Song, Planning for Special Services, Planning for Technology, Thou Shalt Not Steal.*

ISBN: 978-0-939067-79-4

Available from **www.alexanderpublishing.com** or through your local book store.

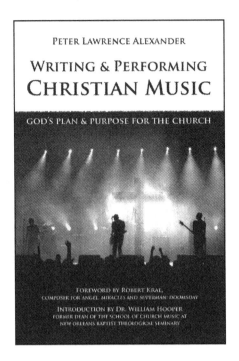

WRITING & PERFORMING CHRISTIAN MUSIC

Peter Lawrence Alexander

Writing and Performing Christian Music: God's Plan & Purpose for the Church, is for songwriters, worship leaders, musicians, composers, church leadership, radio station programmers, and record company executives. Foreword by TV composer Robert Kral (*Angel, Miracles and Superman: Doomsday*). Introduction by Dr. William L. Hooper, former Dean, School of Church Music, New Orleans Baptist Theological Seminary. **Covers:** *What is Christian Music; God's Organizational Model for the Church; The First Formal Purposing of Song; The Prophetic Song; How God Uses Music to Edify; 22 Types of Biblical Songs by Content; Thanks, and the Three Types of Praise Songs; Eight More Types of Biblical Songs; Biblical Techniques of Lyric Writing; Standards and Performance Practices; Music Leadership and the Large Church; Basic Performance Considerations; Wisdom's Role; Picking Music for the Western Church Service.*

ISBN: 978-0-939067-77-0

Available from **www.alexanderpublishing.com** or through your local book store.

APPLIED PROFESSIONAL HARMONY 101

Peter Lawrence Alexander

Applied Professional Harmony 101 is a songwriter and composer's approach to learning harmony. Unlike traditional music courses, you're constantly writing music as you go along. By the end of APH 101 you will have learned how to create a basic demo arrangement of your song. We encourage you to use a MIDI keyboard to get the most out of your work.

"Peter Alexander in his series, Applied Professional Harmony, has created what I feel will be standard text in schools for many years to come. In a thoroughly readable style, he has managed the neat trick of erasing the lines between so called 'popular' music and 'classical' music. Read and Learn."

Henry Mancini

"If I had these books when I was in college, I'd have stayed in music school."

John Tesh

ISBN: 978–0–939067–88–6

CPSIA information can be obtained
at www.ICGtesting.com
Printed in the USA
FSHW020509311220
77298FS